GOLDEN MILESTONE

Golden
Milestone

50 YEARS OF THE AA

EDITED BY

DAVID KEIR

AND

BRYAN MORGAN

THE AUTOMOBILE ASSOCIATION
LONDON

FIRST PUBLISHED IN 1955
by
THE AUTOMOBILE ASSOCIATION
Fanum House London W 1

Produced by
NEWMAN NEAME LIMITED
50 Fitzroy Street London W 1

Printed in Great Britain by
STAPLES PRINTERS LIMITED
Rochester

Designed by
CHARLES HASLER, MSIA

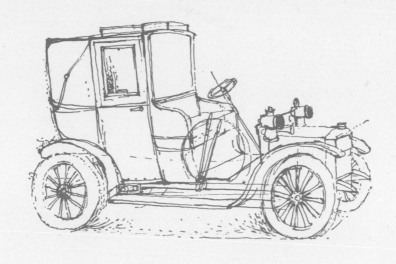

TO ALL THOSE MEMBERS
PAST AND PRESENT
WHO BY THEIR SUPPORT HAVE
ENABLED THE ASSOCIATION
TO EXCEED THE
HOPES AND AMBITIONS
OF ITS FOUNDERS
IN THE CREATION OF
AN IDEAL OF SERVICE

CONTENTS

THE BACKGROUND

THE FOREGROUND

ILLUSTRATIONS

COLOUR PLATES

Plate number : Title : Nearest text page

Colour line drawings will be found between
pages 32 and 33, 104 and 105, 188 and 189, 196 and 197

BLACK AND WHITE PLATES

And seventy-eight line illustrations
distributed throughout the text

ACKNOWLEDGMENTS

Grateful acknowledgment is made to the proprietors of *Punch* for permission to use the cartoons dispersed throughout the book; to the Clerk of the Council, Lynton, for assistance in preparing the map on page 223; and to the following for the loan of prints: the British Museum (the Hereford World Map); Charles Hasler (plate 1, top); Librairie Paul Ollendorff (the Place Vendôme and the pedal tricycle from Uzanne's *La Locomotion dans l'Histoire*); The Parker Gallery (the Mechanical Horse); and the Veteran Car Club of Great Britain (reproductions from *Cooper's Vehicle Journal*, on pages 65 and 79).

Valuable help, in the provision of research facilities, was given by a number of libraries – particularly those of *The Autocar*, London, *The Motor*, and the *News Chronicle* – to the staffs of which thanks are due.

The publishers would like to acknowledge their gratitude to Mr John Cowderoy for his work in taking the colour photographs – with the exception of plates 11, 17 (top), 21, 28, 47 and 53.

Acknowledgment is also made to the following for the use of photographs: Aerofilms Ltd – plates 34 (top), 58 (bottom); *The Autocar*, London – pages 34, 39, plates 3 (middle), 8 (two at top and bottom right), 9 (top), 13 (top), 37 (top left); Baron – facing page 15; G. Douglas Bolton – plates 35 (middle right), 48 (bottom), 49 (top); J. Allan Cash FIBP, FRPS – plate 53; the *Daily Herald* – plate 39 (top); Fox Photos Ltd – plates 32 (top), 36 (bottom left), 44 (top), 54 (bottom left, bottom right), 62 (middle, and bottom right); French Government Tourist Office – plate 54 (bottom centre); German Tourist Information Bureau – plates 51 (bottom), 54 (top left); *The Irish Times* – plate 48 (top); A. F. Kersting AIBP,

FRPS – plate 47; *The Motor* – page 25 and plates 2, 3 (bottom right), 6 (top left), 32 (bottom, second from left); Picture Post Library – plates 1 (bottom), 8 (bottom left), 9 (middle and bottom), 12 (middle), 15 (bottom), 25 (top), 35 (middle left and bottom), 39 (bottom), 45 (top and second from bottom), 46 (top and second from top), 59; Planet News Ltd – plate 54 (top right); Paul Popper Ltd – plates 32 (bottom left), 36 (top three), 40, 41, 54 (two in centre); H. C. Rowley MICE, City Engineer, Norwich – plate 34 (bottom); *The Scotsman* – plates 21, 36 (bottom right); S. Simons AIBP, ARPS – plates 11, 17 (top), 28.

The four-colour process blocks were made by Northern Photo-Engraving Co Ltd, John Swain Ltd and Dalziel Foundry Ltd. Black and white halftones and line blocks were made by Northern Photo-Engraving Co Ltd. Photolitho reproduction of the four-colour line pages was carried out by Phototype Ltd and printed offset litho by D. R. Hillman and Son Ltd.

FOREWORD

The Automobile Association, of which I am privileged to be President, exists for the comfort and help of its Members and to increase the pleasure and safety of all those who use the roads.

Golden Milestone is a combination of the history of the A.A. and a description - sometimes in a light hearted style - of what the A.A. now seeks to accomplish.

I hope that the one and a half million Members will enjoy this book and gain a new insight into this great organisation which is always at their service.

President, Automobile Association.

April, 1955.

INTRODUCTION

By the Chairman of the Automobile Association

CAPTAIN THE RT HON LORD TEYNHAM

DSO, DSC, RN (RTD)

I have been delighted to browse over this book, *Golden Milestone*, not only because it is a history of the A A but because it provides in a delightful manner a panorama of the Association as it is today.

There is almost infinite variety amongst its pages, sometimes serious, sometimes gay, but always making lighthearted and entertaining reading.

Perhaps it would be true to say that it is almost an anthology, to be dipped into at any time, rather than a series to be read solemnly from start to finish.

The chapters in this book have been contributed by many authors and none of them are employees of the Association. If in so doing they have found inspiration from our activities then I think we have not failed in our ideal of service to our members.

Teynham

I. THE EARLY STORY

DAVID KEIR

Under a bright sky in the summer of 1895 the people of Windsor town and castle were startled one day by the strange noise of a petroleum motor carriage. That such a sound should be heard at all seemed almost an affront to the tranquil grandeur of the place. But even more outlandish was the look of the monster; for unmistakably it was a foreigner, though there was nothing foreign about the Honourable Evelyn Ellis who was cheerfully perched at the wheel as if nothing was happening. The townsfolk, on the contrary, were thunderstruck, since it is doubtful if any of them had ever before seen a motor car on the Queen's highway.

What Queen Victoria thought of the Ellis exploit is not recorded. But, if not amused, she must certainly have been amazed. It was only six years since the authorities had banned the public use of a petroleum driven tricycle. And earlier still the Queen had herself signed an Act of Parliament which not only compelled steam driven vehicles to be preceded by a man on foot but limited their speed to four miles an hour in the country and two miles in towns and villages. But now a new issue had arisen. Would these frowning restrictions be enforced against petrol driven machines? None so far had challenged the authorities to give answer on the open road.

Mr Ellis, however, was a man of mettle. For a year or more he had watched France and Germany possess motor cars in plenty while Britain had none, and with kindred spirits he was determined to take up that challenge as a matter of national honour. Accordingly he had shipped his little three and a half horse power Panhard across the Channel and decided to make the Thames his Rubicon.

When he did so the immediate reactions of the police in the Thames valley seemed reassuring. Setting out from London on that glorious June morning, Ellis not only surprised the good folk of Windsor but subsequently drove on to Malvern at an average speed of nearly ten miles an hour. Such progress was clearly beyond the limit prescribed by law, but for once the law was lenient. As Ellis himself said:

'I was very little troubled by the police and they were generally satisfied by my producing my ordinary carriage licence. One old stone breaker threw down his hammer and threw up his arms in amazement as he saw the carriage approaching him, and said: "Well I'm blessed if Mother Shipton's prophecy ain't come true! Here comes a carriage without a horse!"'

But this was in 1895; and less than ten years later, as a result of the increasing popularity of the internal combustion engine, a bitter conflict was under way. To quote an early example, the authorities meted out rough justice to a citizen of Roxburghshire named Elliot who motored one February night in 1896 to Berwick-on-Tweed. Having arrived there at three o'clock in the morning Elliot was, by his own account, picnicing happily in the shadow of the town hall when a posse of thirteen policemen arrived in anything but a picnic mood and briskly had him fined in court for using a horseless carriage without a footman ahead.

However, the motorist won a modest victory later in the year when the government abolished the man on foot and raised the general speed limit to fourteen miles an hour. Strangely enough most people thought the Act also got rid of the hated red flag which the footman usually carried, although in fact the red flag regulation (first imposed in 1865 to regulate steam carriage drivers) had been repealed by a statute of 1878. What was really important was the acceptance of the horseless carriage as part of the British scene.

Furthermore, it soon became a swift and efficient vehicle. To lawyers it was known as a 'mechanical locomotive on the highway' and to horse lovers as an outrage. But nothing could stop its progress. In the first few years of this century automobiles were racing on certain stretches between Paris, Marseilles, Bordeaux and Vienna at the speed of an express train. In Britain the fourteen miles an hour limit was still crippling the motor car industry; but despite this handicap so many new cars kept coming out on the roads that the social life of the country was profoundly affected. This, one Member of Parliament saw very clearly.

Constable (to motorist who has exceeded the speed limit): 'And I have my doubts about this being your first offence. Your face seems familiar to me.'

Speaking at a public dinner in 1905, a young heretic called Churchill remarked that one of the more striking things to his mind was the extraordinary rapidity with which automobilism had overspread national life since the start of the century. 'Five years ago,' he said, 'a motor car was an object of derision if it stopped for one moment; now, the horses have got used to them, the asses have got used to

them, and we see them on every road.' Mr Churchill was too optimistic, for the 1903 *Motor Car Act*'s speed limit of twenty miles an hour
had unfortunately been construed by local constabularies as a means of
prosecuting motorists. Crouching behind the hedgerows now were
policemen, tortured perhaps by flies or possibly enchanted by a pink
mist of wild rose petals showering on their massive shoulders. But in
their hands were stopwatches, and with these instruments of inquisition they waited hungrily for malefactors to enter their measured
furlong at twenty-two and a half, say, instead of twenty miles an hour.

Soon these legitimate prosecutions broadened into persecution.
Soon, too, many motorists began to feel that the place of justice was
less hallowed than they had imagined. At a time when the pound was
worth some six times its present value, the Andover bench raised
£1,000 in a single year; and it was only one of many. There were of
course honourable exceptions – Manchester for instance – but in general there was a widespread bitterness which became open anger
when the stopwatches were sometimes discovered to be untrust-
worthy and the measured distances inaccurate. By 1905, then, there
was enmity on the highways of Britain instead of friendliness, and
motor cars were under a cloud more serious than the white cloud of
dust which generally rose behind them.

In March 1905 *The Autocar* printed a letter about motorists' grievances, written by a young theatrically minded gentleman from
Wolverhampton named Walter Gibbons. Forthrightly Gibbons proposed a club to prevent police traps. He also suggested that cyclists,
wearing special badges and paid from the club's annual subscriptions,
should be engaged to discover the traps and give motorists warning.

As luck would have it a racing driver called Charles Jarrott and his
friend, William Letts, were already operating a private warning
system on certain stretches of the Brighton road: and they naturally
welcomed recruits. By April of that year, indeed, they had roped in a
small group of sympathisers, and only a few weeks later they were in
a position to call themselves the Automobile Mutual Association.

Events now moved fast. On 26th June the executive of this body casually decided to call itself the Automobile Association, and a day later an appeal for recruits was posted to the motoring periodicals. Unfortunately the first answers to the appeal were as dusty as the roads of the time. *The Motor*, for example, saw any system to warn motorists of police traps as 'a proceeding of questionable dignity' and suggested that the 'published propaganda of the new association' could best be dealt with by the already established Motor Union. The A A enthusiasts, of course, did not believe a word of all this: they had suffered on the roads too long and without redress. But they lacked a pivot for their ideas.

At this stage in the story a rather depressed young man of thirty was standing alone one evening in Shaftesbury Avenue. As a salesman in a small way he should by rights have been homeward bound for Highbury and the company of his wife, but most of his recent days had been so profitless that he watched the buses go by with a feeling of disquiet. Would his present ill luck continue, he wondered, or was there a tide in the affairs of men for people of thirty?

As he stood on the pavement in this dismal mood, there flashed into his mind the name of Charles Gulliver, a lawyer friend to whom he owed a small sum of money. Feeling that he ought to explain to his friend (and creditor) that the spirit was still willing though the bank was weak he went off to Fleet Street, where Gulliver worked in the office of a lawyer named Amery-Parkes who was lending office space to the newly formed A A. But of this the young man was as ignorant as his interest in automobiles was slight. Gloomily he got off the bus and made for 18 Fleet Street in the hope that his friend Gulliver had not yet gone home.

He need hardly have worried. As temporary honorary secretary of the A A, Gulliver was pondering the problem of a paid successor to himself at the very moment when that depressed young man in vague search of a job walked through the front door and gave his name as Stenson Cooke.

When Stenson Cooke, almost by hazard, was appointed Secretary of the Association in the last week of August 1905 he knew that his tenure of office in a small and struggling organisation was bound to be precarious. But, as it turned out, he was the right man for the A A because the A A was the right kind of organisation for Stenson Cooke. In an older and more stereotyped enterprise he might have been less effective, but as it was he threw himself with tremendous zest into his new duties, though his early path was difficult. He knew nothing whatsoever about motor cars and was unaccustomed to a committee way of life. Yet in one sense his very ignorance was bliss, for he brought a fresh eye to bear not only on the problems of the road but on the organisation he was to serve devotedly for so many years.

There were shocks for the new Secretary, however, the first being in the shape of the following dispatch from the battlefield:

'I think you will find the patrolling of the Brighton road last fortnight has been carried out to the Association's instructions with the exception of the four Brighton men of which I have not seen the last fortnight but I believe you will find those men have not turned up because they were not paid. I have written to these men but failed to get an answer but if you think it necessary to get fresh men I will do so.'

There may have been an oversight here, or there may have been some trouble with the missing road scouts which is now hidden in Edwardian mists. But at least the letter emphasised the need for a permanent official with an eye for detail. It was, indeed, the eye for detail of that £150 a year man, working in a single room with a borrowed typewriter and his accounts in arrears, which made him realise that the Association needed a telegraphic address. On the very day he received

PLATE 1

*At the beginning
of the nineteenth century
the horse
was reigning unchallenged
over a glamorous
coaching age . . .*

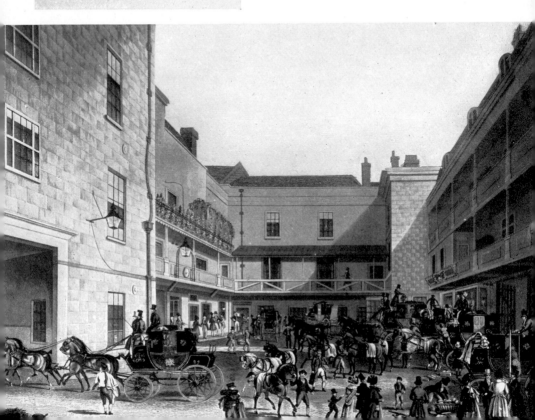

. . . but before that century was out the roads had been invaded by
such machines as this *Panhard*, which for all its amateurish-looking gears (*below*)
was the first horseless carriage successfully to tour *Britain*.

PLATE 2

the disturbing note about the missing scouts he picked at random from a Post Office list the phrase 'Fanum, London'.

Being gifted with tremendous energy, the new Secretary was soon in his stride. And fortunately his task was eased a little by the fact that, a few days before his appointment, a meeting of the committee had given the A A a settled pattern. Colonel W. J. Bosworth, in private life a military tutor, was elected Chairman, with Sir Archibald Macdonald as his vice-chairman. A popular Anglo-German named Ludwig Schlentheim became honorary treasurer, and the committee included Walter Gibbons, Charles Jarrott, Selwyn Francis Edge, Earl Russell the barrister, and Alfred King-Hamilton (who was still giving his counsel to the Association in its golden jubilee year).

Contemporary drawings of Stenson Cooke and Colonel W. J. Bosworth.

The pace of events now quickened. All through the summer of 1905 motorists had been afflicted with a spate of prosecutions, as 18 Fleet Street knew only too well. In one of the very first letters he opened,

C

Stenson Cooke was told by a new member that since one of the Brighton road patrols had saved him from a police trap he had sent in two grateful guineas. Unfortunately, like Sir Arthur Conan Doyle and many others before him, he had been caught on the road to Portsmouth. So could not the A A extend its activities there?

Though such an expansion was not easy for a young organisation, the committee at the beginning of September threw down its gauntlet on that historic highway: and by mid-month cycle patrols were operating between Kingston and Godalming. This of course meant increased friction between the A A and the police, for as soon as a trap was discovered the patrols in their yellow armlets were there and the wise motorist accordingly reduced his speed.

Here let us look forward a month. On 23rd October *The Times* published the following communiqué from Stenson Cooke:

'I have the pleasure to inform motorists that the heavily trapped part of the Portsmouth road, from Esher to the nineteenth milestone, will henceforth be patrolled by our cyclist scouts on every day of the

week. This is our first step towards that daily protection which it is
the aim of our committee to establish and, funds permitting, continue
on every important road, until the time shall arrive when police traps
cease from troubling, and the stopwatch is at rest.'

Studied in silhouette against the road confusion of the previous
month, this bold announcement is seen to be one of the most daring
in the Association's history. It was only a few weeks since one of its
members had been stopped by the police on the Fairmile stretch of the
Portsmouth road and accused of exceeding the speed limit. When the
case came into court a mere four days before Stenson Cooke's battle
cry, a scout swore he had followed the car for some time on a bicycle
and that it was certainly not travelling at more than fifteen or sixteen
miles an hour. The motorist, too, was equally convinced that the
police had gravely over estimated his speed. In the end the police
evidence was accepted and the driver was fined £5 with costs.

To the anxious committee this news was sombre, since for the
first time one of their scouts was involved in a legal case; and from

the start the members, though militant, were anxious not to have their scouts humiliated. For that very reason some of the committee had doubted the wisdom of putting the patrol in the witness box at all. They knew, of course, that if his evidence was accepted by the bench the A A's star would be high in the ascendant: but if on the other hand he were disbelieved then its reputation for integrity would be tarnished. So the dismal effect of the result can be imagined. But the committee's cup was not yet full. Several weeks later, news came through that the patrol had been thrown into Brixton gaol on a charge of committing wilful and corrupt perjury. The whole future of the Association was suddenly and dramatically at stake.

Reassembled in the Fleet Street office, the anxious committeemen decided to fight to the end, despite the fact that new members were still coming in at the rate of only ten a month and that they themselves would probably have to dip their hands into their pockets. Luckily, that little room never lacked courage; the case was fought with the aid of a KC, the learned committeeman Earl Russell, and a third

counsel; and after a lusty legal battle at Guildford Assizes it was won.

Even so it was to be some time before the motor car was generally accepted, and for this a romantic animal was to blame. Until the self propelled vehicle came along, road traffic had always moved at the speed of the horse – and the horse itself was accustomed to sharing the road with some two million of its own kind. It was thus hardly surprising that horse owners were provoked to fury when horseless carriages appeared abruptly round corners hitherto unsullied and frightened animals became unmanageable.

Walkers, too, were vocal when their enjoyment was disturbed on a sunny day by clouds of dust falling on the high midsummer pomps of the countryside, but in the end it was the horsemen and those who made their livelihood from the animal in one way or other who were responsible for most of the early prejudice against the automobile. For centuries, after all, landowners had bred and pastured horses, dealers had sold them, harness makers had equipped them, grain merchants had helped to keep them fed and coach makers had turned out the vehicles which kept them busy. There was, in fact, a compound vested interest behind the animal when the motor car dropped like a thunderbolt among the quiet lanes of the British countryside.

At the end of 1905 the committee naturally felt that the Fairmile case
had been a splendid Christmas present. But, like many other kinds of
gift, this one had to be paid for: and who was to pay?

On 2nd January 1906, when the committee met in Fleet Street, the
cost of the case was the main item on the agenda; and this, said
Amery-Parkes the solicitor, would not be less than £260. The Association, however, was overdrawn at the bank; new members were
coming in too slowly for comfort; and the committee had been forced
to increase its expenditure by taking on a typist and an office boy
(who promptly absconded with some £8 of petty cash). None the
less their mood was cheerful. Let us have a big dinner, they said,
which will bring in some of the money required and get the Association useful publicity as well.

Later in the month the dinner at the Trocadero was duly held, with
famous artists and a menu which speaks for itself. It was suggested
that each guest should be handed a card inviting a contribution to the
Fairmile expenses. This appeal was successful, since it brought in
£360 – which, along with a gift of fifty guineas from the Society of
Motor Manufacturers and Traders, enabled the Association to get
out of its dark wood and face the rest of the year with confidence.

The battle for the open road was meanwhile as fierce as ever. In
the south the scouts were still hotfoot on the way to Brighton. To the
west a victory had just been won on the Portsmouth road. But the
north looked suddenly cold and threatening, since for some time
there had been frequent appeals for assistance on the Great North
road. Accordingly patrols were organised in January 'as far as the
twenty-fifth milestone'; and a little later Stenson Cooke was directed
'to go to Buckden at an early date to complete arrangements'.

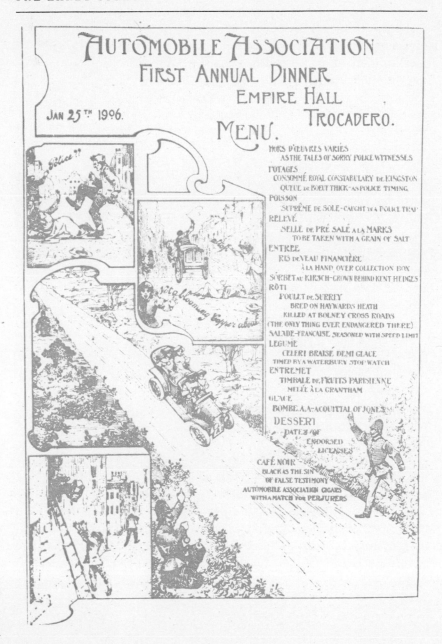

There is the smack of a secret plot about all this. But in fact the arrangements were as open as sunlight on a dark road. At a previous meeting, after Earl Russell had denounced the Buckden trap in Huntingdonshire, the committee had decided to erect a big public notice warning all motorists of the trap's existence. For cool daring, in the heated temper of the time, this proposal would be hard to rival. None the less it was carried through. Stenson Cooke hired space for the warning board from a Buckden cowkeeper at an annual cost of a guinea, and by May it not only stood in its place but set the fashion for similar warnings elsewhere.

As we look back on those stormy days it is remarkable how ingeniously the first committee and its Secretary waged what almost resembled a military campaign. It is also striking to note how conscientiously the patrols carried out their work, though some were prosecuted from time to time for 'obstructing the police in the execution of their duties' and cycle transport during inclement weather could not have been pleasant.

'Beyond Guildford,' wrote a reporter from *The Motor* around this time, 'the country was covered with about two inches of snow. This not only made the running very heavy, but our discomfort was added to by snow falling heavily. Despite this the A A scout was still at his work, alert as ever, and by his timely warning in the fast falling snow saved a hurrying motorist and blasted the hopes of two policemen who had come so far afield thinking to pounce, in the dim light, on a car hastening home.'

Reverting to the committeemen's own imaginative planning, they now equipped their senior patrols with field glasses and provided badges for their cyclists. One side of these circular discs bore the letters 'A A' in yellow on a white background to signify 'all clear'; but if the police were active the discs were reversed so that motorists could see the same letters in black against red and drive as delicately as Agag would have done had Agag been a member. There were, however, some motorists whose glee in accepting the patrols' warnings

Before powered vehicles
appeared on the scene,
some strange hobby horses
invaded the roads.

The upper of
these illustrations shows
an English model of 1830:
the lower,
a more recent comment
on the subject.

"Of course this means the end of the horse."

But at the same time men were designing horseless carriages.
The plans of the 1820s were sometimes of an over-traditional character.

MESSRS. BURSTALL AND HILL'S EDINBURGH STEAM CARRIAGE.

Even then, however, workable steam carriages were
on the road. Examples are these – both of about 1827.

MR. GURNEY'S LONDON STEAM CARRIAGE, AS IT APPEARED IN
THE REGENTS PARK, ON THURSDAY, DECEMBER
6, 1827.

was only equalled by their reluctance to pay two guineas to the
patrols' employers. This attitude was dealt with in two ways.

Firstly the committee decided that their scouts should only assist
Association members; and, secondly, paid up members were given a
badge which soon became a talisman inspiring its owners with a feeling of fraternity and collective security. On this score Stenson Cooke
has an amusing vignette in his memoirs of what used to happen when
A A badges, looking much the same as they do now, began to sprout
from an ever increasing number of cars.

'Look!' said a member's wife. 'There's a car in front with Our
Badge on – he's being saluted by Our Man. Nice, eh? Our turn next.
Ooh! Here we are. Go on, return the salute. NO! not with your left
hand, silly! Right hand – and take your cigar out of your mouth.'

Badges, in fact, became the order of the day; for as the months went
on and the Association began to turn friendly garages and motor repair shops into an additional flanking force these too were given a
badge – in the shape, this time, of a flag pole. The enticement was
simple, but clever in its very simplicity. Members were told to
patronise garages with the flag pole above the door; and in return the
garages used the poles to warn the motorist of any trap in their
vicinity. If the local police were active a yellow ball was drawn up to
the top of the flag pole, whereupon the motorist was expected to stop
and ask the garage for 'the message'. In most cases he got a verbal
warning of the trap ahead, but as the system spread from pole to pole
he sometimes got messages of quite another kind – that a member of
his family had just met with an accident, maybe, and that he should
therefore return at once.

Almost without realising it the Association was becoming a social
service: and it was perhaps for this very reason that it suddenly began
to expand. At the annual meeting in mid-June membership was over
900. By the end of the year, when it was nearly 3,000, the A A was
on the brink of one of the most astonishing growths in the history of
British institutions. And by good fortune it was during this growth

that the committee began to take a long sighted view of the future.
They saw many old opponents shedding their prejudices, a fact
largely due to the Association's pluck and enterprise having attracted some of the usual admiration that greets the small chap fighting
the big 'un. Was he too small after all, some wondered, or would his
clever ringcraft tell in the end? The answer was soon forthcoming.
For although the A A had been cradled in conflict its founders were
now to foster the idea of service in a wider and more fruitful field than
that of guerilla warfare with the police.

In the New Year of 1907 it was difficult for the motoring world to foretell the shape of things to come; and even Old Moore was of little help, since all that weatherbeaten prophet could see ahead for the motoring community was a possible dust tax on motor cars, a tip subsequently proved as shaky as his expectation of earthquakes in the midlands. He certainly never prophesied (nor assessed the importance of) the A A's move in April to the Leicester Square area. But as it turned out a great many of the tentative ideas discussed during the winter of 1907 began to take shape with such speed that the five years which followed became the Automobile Association's great seminal period. Let us look at them more closely.

At the beginning of 1907 that motoring enthusiast, King Edward VII, was visiting his friends by Daimler. Such a cachet for the motor car was important at the time, and may have contributed to the Association's sharp membership rise from 300 to 3,000 during the previous year. It was encouraging, too, that the erection of the first village sign at Hatfield at the end of 1906 paved the way for the first danger signs in the summer, the first school signs in the autumn, and the first direction signs two years later. But the whole year was rich in constructive effort. At small cost members were offered legal assistance should they come before a magistrate. A special policy of insurance was arranged through Lloyds. A service of local guides was instituted for the benefit of members passing through large towns. Motor cyclists were admitted to membership. And, finally, the Association opened its first branch office – at Manchester – and put patrols on the main roads of Lancashire and Yorkshire.

In the light of such progress the committee should have felt happier about the future. But unfortunately their relations with a rival organisation, the Motor Union, were bedevilled by disputes which weakened the motorists' cause at a critical time.

The trouble started in the spring, when the Motor Union began to distribute badges to its members. Most members of the A A committee saw this as an infringement of copyright, so to speak, and protested loudly. In particular they complained that the initials 'M U' were arranged in the Motor Union's badge much as its own letters were by the Automobile Association; and indeed it was soon proved that patrols found approaching cars difficult to distinguish.

THIS ENVELOPE IS TO CONTAIN THE ROAD CARDS, WHICH SHOULD ALWAYS BE CARRIED BY MEMBERS WHEN MOTORING.

A.A. Patrols wear a Circular Metal Badge lettered **A.A.** (with a number) in YELLOW and WHITE on one side, and similarly in BLACK and RED on the other side.

In future The Patrols' signals are to be interpreted as follows :—

White Side of Badge and Military Salute means I am here if you want me.

RED SIDE and Military Salute means Please drive more carefully.

RED SIDE, holding Right Hand Straight above the Head means STOP PLEASE.

Members are asked to report all cases of incivility or inattention on the part of Patrols to the Secretary, giving date, time and place and number of Patrol.

However, these spring protests were only April showers compared with the August thunder which rolled round the Motor Union's later decision to station 'road agents' as a warning to drivers of dangerous places, and (as they claimed) 'to advise motorists when driving through villages and towns where special caution is necessary'. Since these agents – recruited mainly from retired police sergeants and constables – were to wear a cap, belt and armlet, confusion was about to be so much worse confounded that the Association launched further protests. In one of these Colonel Bosworth suggested that the Motor Union's main function was to handle legislative difficulties on behalf of the motorist, and that with this necessary duty the Automobile Association had never interfered. But to put new agents on the road would merely duplicate the Association's work.

The Motor Union's reply was that their road agents would only work in towns and villages, which provoked a characteristic thrust from Stenson Cooke. 'The Automobile Association,' he said, 'was originally called into existence by the public demand for what the Motor Union and other bodies did not do; and its instantaneous success proved the great need for it. Success, however, has its sorrows as well as adversity, and brain picking, unfortunately, is a thing which can never be legislated against.' But the storm passed as all storms do, and eventually the Motor Union not only agreed to modify its badge but withdrew its road guides. Peace reigned again.

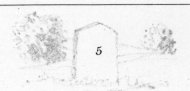

5

Yet at the beginning of 1908 the public relations of the motorist were still untidy. Because a number of reckless drivers were still riding rough wheeled over other people's feelings, the motorist's genuine grievances were often misunderstood or misrepresented both in the press and among the public; and the Association was bound to share this obloquy, though it does not seem to have shed its wisdom. For some time it had realised that unless the road hog was curbed police traps would be extended, further restrictions imposed, and the twenty miles an hour speed limit made permanent. In particular it had begun to consider that the scouts' display of the white 'all clear' side of their disc was merely encouraging the speed maniacs. Once realised, this situation was met. Early in January the patrols were instructed to display only the red side of the disc (when danger lay ahead) – and, equally important, they were to interpret danger as meaning not only police traps but all other hazards on the road: a herd of cattle, say, a blind corner or a traction engine at work.

Heartened by the compliments it received for this sensible step, the Association in May launched its Committee of Public Safety. This body's main functions were to keep the patrols informed of cars which were being driven inconsiderately, to request the resignation of members who were persistent offenders, to report non-members to their own motor clubs or societies, and even to report unattached motorists to the police as incorrigible if they continued to offend. By these imposing tokens the Association clearly meant business; but business there had to be. For already a new spate of scorching had heartened the 'hedgehogs', as motorists dubbed the police.

In March of 1909, indeed, Colonel Bosworth had been optimistic enough to declare at the annual meeting that the A A's relations with

POLICE-TIMED ROADS.

We invite our readers to advise us
of any police activity which may come
under their observation, to enable us
to keep the map corrected up to date.
The reference key giving the exact
situation of the numbered traps on the
map will be found on the opposite
page.

*On 18th May 1907 'The Autocar' published its first map
of existing police traps.*

the police became pleasanter as it grew older. What he probably did not know when he made his speech was the wording of a general order issued a fortnight earlier by Captain Sant, the chief of the Surrey constabulary: 'Whenever a motor scout is found warning motorists of the presence of the police and of the existence of a measured distance, his name and address is to be taken and sent to this office with a report of the circumstances for my information'.

The meaning of this was as clear as Captain Sant's offensive was deliberate. For all through that spring, summer and autumn the Surrey constabulary showed unusual determination, until at one stage it almost seemed as irked by the sun-seeking motorists on the Hog's Back as Tibetans are irritated by sunburned faces.

Captain Sant's attack began early. On the usual charge of obstructing the police he had one scout summoned, and in evidence it was stated that this scout had been 'jumping about the road waving his pocket handkerchief, exhibiting the red side of his badge and shouting "Police".' The scout was fined £2 with £5 costs. The committee, not surprisingly, was exasperated by this case, since a few months earlier it had dismissed one patrol who had been convicted for foolishly standing in the middle of a measured distance and deliberately obscuring a constable's view.

By this time, then, the Surrey roads were seething with ill temper: for the war had become one of attrition, and both sides – the public force and the private commando – were becoming more dogged. So too were the local magistrates, who were levying savage fines incommensurate with purely technical offences. A new gun had therefore to be pulled out of the Association's armoury; and, as it turned out, this weapon had considerable fire power. In the month of August, when holiday traffic was at its height, the Association advised its members to boycott certain Surrey districts altogether. Hotels, repairers, tradesmen were not to be patronised; establishment licences, gun licences and motor car registrations were not to be taken out in the county; and members were even asked to draw the attention of house agents to the diminished demand for property in Surrey if Surrey became unfit for motorists to live in.

But though this long guerilla campaign was exhausting it did not distract the Association from constructive work. Apart from the £6,000 expended on patrols alone between May 1907 and March 1908, money was spent on hundreds of road signs. A foreign touring department was created to meet what had quickly become a vital need. And the first of a series of handbooks was published 'to acquaint the members with all the facilities and arrangements now existing for their benefit on the road'. The hotels now appointed by the AA were provided with special bulletin boards – each with a locked cabinet – giving 'exclusive road information', the nature of which may be guessed. Across the border an office was opened in Glasgow and the number of patrols was increased in certain Scottish counties; for in Scotland, as later in Ireland, the Association started operations at the request of indigenous motorists who wished to enjoy the same benefits as did members in England. By the end of 1908 membership was more than 9,000.

D

In the story of most institutions there is some memorable event which with the years takes on a mellow glitter of its own; and for the Automobile Association this took place on 17th March 1909, when it transported a fully equipped Guards battalion from London to Hastings and back. It sounds a simple undertaking today; but for the time it was a startling feat, since no logistic precedents existed in this country for the use of automobiles on such a scale. That apart, the popular interest aroused by the expedition helped to improve the still uneasy relations between motorists and the public at large.

The original idea of moving troops by mechanised means was put up to the army by the Association itself. For some time, in its new resolve that skirmishing with policemen should be subordinate to the twin ideals of providing a first class service to members and securing greater respect for motorists in general, the committee had felt the need for a convincing proof of the motor car's potentialities; and here it was at last. To ensure the scheme's success the A A enlisted the help of the M P for Hastings, who in turn persuaded the Secretary of State for War to arrange for the services of a Guards battalion.

Soon the arrangements were going forward in an atmosphere of expectancy – and of lightheartedness as well, for the run was to take place on St Patrick's Day and the Mayor of Hastings had promised the guardsmen Irish stew for lunch. As for the drivers, Stenson had thought up a typically ingenious device: they were to be accommodated in groups at A A appointed hotels. But the highlight of the authorities' arrangements was their instruction to all police inspectors on the London-Hastings road to co-operate not only with the battalion of Guards *en route* but with the patrols who would then be out in force.

Everyone was hence in good humour when the cavalcade set off from its assembly point and made its way through large crowds from the Crystal Palace. And indeed the whole affair from beginning to end was a triumphal progress for guardsmen and AA alike, with masses turning out everywhere along the route and the newspapers printing reports as flattering as the Army Council's praise for the 'public spirited generosity' of the 'large and influential portion of the community whom the Automobile Association may be regarded as representing'. When the Secretary of State himself was also laudatory the AA seemed to be surrounded by sweetness and light. But there were unsettling undertones.

To understand the new anxieties we must look back to 1907. In that year a scout called Little was acquitted on a charge of wilfully obstructing a constable in the execution of his duty. In the Court of Appeal the judgment in favour of the patrol was upheld, which was especially satisfactory since the Association's case had rested on a claim that the patrol, ahead of the trap, was merely warning all passing motorists to go slow; there was no question of his warning those *inside* the trap to save them from the consequences of their law breaking, nor was he physically obstructing the constable.

With a new case in the autumn of 1909, however, the legality of the patrol's warning again became an issue. Earlier that year a patrol named Betts had passed a group of police officers near the top of a hill outside Guildford, and after taking up his position several hundred yards away he had displayed the red side of his badge. Unhappily for Betts, the police had developed a new tactical sense. While he was cheerfully protecting the pockets of his members, the police were altering their measured distances till finally (according to their evidence) Betts was caught delivering a warning *inside* the trap. In court he was convicted and fined for obstructing the police, as many patrols had been before him. But this time the Association appealed, and in the Court of Appeal their counsel made the point strongly that the patrol was only doing the same thing as the police – namely,

checking excessive speed. The bench (composed of two judges who
confessed to A A membership and a third who denied being a member
but became one a year or two later) decided against the patrol, and
therefore against the existing system of organised warnings. It
seemed to many motorists as great a disaster as the Fairmile case had
been a triumph.

The committee fortunately had planned for disaster as well as its
fellow impostor, triumph. On the very day of the lost appeal the
following notice was posted to all members:

TO A A MEMBERS

WHEN A PATROL DOES

NOT SALUTE

STOP

AND ASK THE *REASON*

Resilient and daring as ever, the committee thus faced the authorities with a new tactic – which, according to Stenson Cooke's
memoirs, worked something like this:

'Good morning, sir!'

'Good-er-hm! When a patrol does not salute, stop and – that's it –
why *didn't* you?'

'It's quite all right, sir. Lucky you did stop, you were going a comfortable thirty, and' (*whispering*) 'they're at it half a mile ahead, sir.'

'They're . . . '

'Yes, sir, trapping! Caught seven already they have; but none of
Ours.'

'Ooh! Thanks awfully, jolly fine! Good luck to the A A Badge!'

'Yes, sir, but remember, *you must stop*. We can't tell you anything
unless you stop – see?'

By good fortune a batch of legal cases towards the end of 1909 was
decided in favour of the Association, which somehow always seemed
able in the stormy years to give itself a Christmas present. For instance, at the end of November a patrol named Joy was summoned for
obstructing the police. In evidence it was said that Joy had stationed

himself beside the control while the police were timing cars over a
measured distance of two miles, and that, as the result of his warning,
many cars which would have been trapped slowed down. The view of
the A A lawyer was that the evidence of speed at the time the warning
was given was not sufficient to justify a conviction; and this was
accepted by the bench. So Joy was unconfined.

The effect of these successes was so remarkable that, when the
year ended, the Association could boast 12,000 members. Nevertheless, legal victories alone were insufficient to attract new members in
such a flood, though the setting up of a free legal defence department
during the year attracted many waverers. But 1909 was a notable
year in many other respects. For the first time superintendents appeared on the roads to supervise the patrols: the first danger signs
went up near crossroads and concealed drives: the first illuminated
sign was erected at Cobham; and there were two capital gains – a
branch office in Paris, and a London move to more spacious premises
at Whitcomb Street.

The calendar for 1910 showed no abatement of imagination or of
energy. Abroad, in the New Year, the Association's story was told to
a still wider world at two automobile exhibitions in New York. At
home, it opened branch offices in Liverpool, Dublin and Belfast.

The expansion in Ireland is particularly noteworthy because bad
roads and indifferent hotels had prompted many Irish motorists to
urge the Association to extend into their country. Thus a staff of
officials crossed the Irish Sea, not only to erect road signs and continuous milestones in a countryside where both were lacking and to
arrange with shipping companies for the easy transhipment of members' cars, but to consider the appointment of garages and hotels.
(These often lacked such amenities as brushes, combs and hand towels
until the A A introduced cabinets containing them, as it had already
done in certain parts of England.) The signs, too, went up apace, so
that by 1914 – when some 3,000 had been erected – it was rather
easier for the stranger to find his way to Ballymuck and Ballybunion,
or even to Dublin and Belfast. But in the end it was the condition of
the roads which demanded most care and thought from the Association's chief fugleman in Ireland, a spirited and witty Irishman named
Arthur Allen who later became touring manager in London and the
A A's representative on the Alliance Internationale de Tourisme.
Patrols in Ireland were not particularly required at this stage, the
main issue being to rouse interest in the need for decent roads. To
that end almost thirty road committees were formed, with a total
honorary membership of more than 2,000 road users of all kinds; and
these were unsparing in their propaganda.

During this fight for better roads – and bigger government grants
for Irish road development – England, Scotland and Wales were

naturally not neglected. The illuminated road signs which had begun to appear at the end of 1909 were increased in number. The insurance department made progress with a special policy covering almost every kind of risk. On a higher policy plane, the Association was granted a privilege of some importance when it gained authority to issue an international pass and fix identification plates on foreign-bound cars. Yet, important as all these events were, they were overshadowed by a major act of policy at the end of 1910 which virtually transformed the motoring scene.

For at least a year the suggestion had been constantly made by motorists that three protective organisations with London head-quarters (the Royal Automobile Club, the Motor Union and the Association itself) were too many, and at this point fate took a hand. In early summer William Rees Jeffreys, the Secretary of the Motor Union, went to another post and tongues wagged vigorously. A union between the A A and the Motor Union would be easier, they said, now that the chief Motor Union architect was out of the way. Then, in August, Colonel Bosworth (who had been laid up by a stroke in the spring) was forced to resign his Chairmanship of the Automobile Association, and a rival architect had been removed. Soon there were private conversations between leading members of both bodies, which proved so cordial that by mid-November a fusion agreement was reached. In the last week of that month the event was made public, together with the names of the new office holders.

The Automobile Association and Motor Union, as the new body was called for a time, chose its leaders wisely. As President they had that much loved sportsman, the Earl of Lonsdale. The new Chairman, who had already been Chairman of the Motor Union, was William Joynson-Hicks. In the election of vice-chairman there was another fitting division of honours: Sir Archibald MacDonald of the A A generously proposed that he should retire to make the negotiations easier, but he was shouted down and became vice-chairman of the new body in company with C. H. Dodd of the Motor Union. In the same way, Schlentheim of the AA and Ballin Hinde of the MU were appointed joint honorary treasurers. An executive committee, consisting of eight members from each of the two bodies, included the Reverend F. W. Hassard-Short, Charles McWhirter, Walter Gibbons, Alfred King-Hamilton and Charles Jarrott. Stenson Cooke became the new Secretary as a matter of course – and was at once nicknamed Extension Cooke. And, to look ahead, there is ample proof that the amalgamation was harmonious, since the MU was to supply not only the present but a future Chairman of the new AA in Hassard-Short, and two future Secretaries of merit – Edward Fryer and William Gibson.

Above all, the new membership was 28,040 and looked like increasing. Even so, not one of the negotiators could have guessed that, once their *pax automobilica* was signed, new members would join at the rate of 1,000 each month.

And so in 1911 – one of the most remarkable years in its history – the extended AA swung easily into its new stride. Within a few weeks its Chairman was urging road authorities to deal with the menace of widespreading uncut hedges, and a little later it brought successful court actions against boys who threw stones at motor vehicles and against van drivers who deliberately obstructed members' cars. Finally, the Glamorgan county council was made to pay damages to a member, one of whose car wheels had sunk into a hole improperly filled after a road subsidence.

Truly the wheel of fortune which had spun so often against the Association in its struggling days was now turning in its favour, for the whole of 1911 glittered with signs of progress. The astounding increase in membership throughout the year was no more than a recognition of work being done. To take a month or two at random; in May the executive committee elected more than 900 new members; in August Princess Louise, Duchess of Argyll, Prince Maurice of Battenberg, the Duc d'Orléans, Sir Edward Grey and a host of other famous figures appeared among the 1,748 motorists elected;

PLATE 3

*The A A was born out of
conflict and controversy.
The warning signal
outside a garage (just in
front of the middle window, above),
and the friendly word of a
part-time road scout (right),
were the early motorist's
defence against
police persecution (below).*

PLATE 4

*From a small room in a
solicitor's office (above),
the Association expanded
until it occupied a building
on its present
Leicester Square site (left).*

*Today its nationwide coverage
is symbolised by the
random selection of
area offices shown opposite —
Birmingham, Edinburgh, Cardiff
Guildford, Leeds, Truro
Reading and Southampton*

PLATE 5

In the days when Stenson Cooke's own A A badge was new, the officers included

such enthusiasts as the
Earl of Lonsdale (top)
and the Rev Canon
Hassard-Short (left,
in a later photograph).

PLATE 6

and in September the future Earl of Birkenhead joined with 775
others. That Winston Churchill also became a member during 1911
was only what one would expect in such a vintage year.

But let us take a quick windscreen view of other advances. Branch
offices were opened at Birmingham and Leeds. The patrols (who were
now wearing blue peaked caps with yellow piping and an A A badge
on the front) were supplied with first aid outfits and given a course of
instruction. An industrial vehicle section was started to give commercial firms the privileges enjoyed by private members. Facilities
with the Motor Union Insurance Company were arranged and the
old badge was given the surmounting wings of the Union which are
so familiar today.

Yet somehow, though the auspices seemed so favourable, the Association never did have it the easy way. While it was co-operating
with administrative authority so successfully, legal authority was still
obstructive. Scotland bristled with police traps; and farther south, in
the summer quarter of the year, the Kingston-on-Thames county jus-
tices netted some £300 in motorists' fines. But authority did not
always have its own way. When Harrogate corporation sought
power to make charges for water used in the washing of motor cars,
the Association was roused to such strong opposition that the proposal was withdrawn. Many applications by local authorities for low
speed limits in allegedly populous places were successfully resisted.
As for cyclists (who had become a nocturnal menace as they pedalled
along without lights, to the danger of themselves and the overtaking
motorist), the Association made a public offer of 10,000 free red
reflectors to the first who cared to apply.

In 1912 the flow of new members was so astonishing that in April
alone a record number of 2,691 was enrolled and the membership
exceeded 43,000. Furthermore, recruits were varied enough to include Mr Asquith, the Archbishop of Canterbury and scores of
Smiths, Joneses and Browns. As the number of members grew, so too
did the branch offices. Hotel starring began and, finally, to complete
the record of an impressive year, the first of the telephone boxes
for patrols was erected in July on the Ashford-Hythe road.

The appeal of the roadside boxes was great from the beginning, if
only because they gave motorists a new sense of security and could
be used for purposes far beyond simple telephone calls to garage or
hotel. Patrolmen, for example, now used them for the transmission
of the weather reports which were started earlier in the year. And
luckily their advent coincided with a new phase of improved relations
with the authorities.

But though 1912 ended with a happy Christmas air of peace and goodwill, 1913 opened on a jarring note – and in no less a place than Shakespeare's country. At the end of January the Association had a Warwickshire farmer summoned for assaulting a patrol and using obscene language. For some time the patrol, with police connivance, had been helping to regulate traffic at the East Gate of Warwick, till one day the farmer drove a cart through on the wrong side of the road. The patrol signalled him to keep on his correct side; but instead of showing gratitude the farmer suddenly turned and drove his horse and cart at the patrol to the tune of certain phrases which would make for ill will anywhere. Hence the action which the Association brought – not, as its advocate said, vindictively, but simply to bring home to the defendant that he should in the public interest keep to the rules of the road and not obstruct the patrol in carrying out his duties. The use of the word 'duties' here is very interesting; but its implication was certainly accepted by the Warwick magistrates, for after fining the farmer for a technical assault they expressed the hope that the public would 'co-operate with the Association in the useful work which it is doing on the road'.

Assuredly the times had changed: but changing, too, were the relations between police and patrols. In the first few months of the year at least half a dozen stolen cars were traced by the patrol network. It was also noticeable by this time that the long struggle to curb reckless driving had so reduced the number of road hogs (and thereby diminished the prejudice of most non-motorists) that the Home Secretary could in July make an announcement which most motorists thought historic. In a circular issued to police authorities, Reginald McKenna said decisively that police traps could only be recommended where high speeds were really dangerous. One feels that the chiefs of the A A must have drunk a special little toast not only to McKenna but to their own 70,000 members when they heard of this latest victory in the long battle for the open road.

Hence at the beginning of 1914 the horizons of the Association seemed bright with promise. It is true that the recklessness of a few road hogs had brought about a new rash of police traps in London, that the Chief Constable of Brecknockshire was about to complain of carelessly driven cars in his domain and invite the A A's co-operation in stopping the nuisance, and that a number of members were complaining of over festive drivers in South Wales. But these were minor blots on an otherwise glowing escutcheon.

From Ireland (where a Cork office had been opened in the previous year) came heartening news that the local authorities had been persuaded to spend an extra £30,000 on road improvement. In the south of France the Association secured Riviera headquarters at the Nice Automobile Club. At home the membership rose to nearly 83,000; and headquarters, as full of ideas as ever, had taken over the traffic arrangements for Goodwood races and a great many other sporting and agricultural events. The A A was even running a persuasive campaign to stop its members from tooting their motor horns outside churches on Sundays when suddenly Europe was darkened by the murder of an Austrian archduke at Sarajevo.

THE EARLIEST EXAMPLE OF WOOD ENGRAVING
FOR ILLUSTRATION

This picture of St Christopher, made in 1423 and found in a convent near Augsburg in Germany, shows the traditional protector of all who travel, who lodge at inns or need assistance on their way. It is reproduced at this halfway point in the history of the Automobile Association as a reminder that succour for all who make journeys has ancient and honourable roots.

As many of us know from our own experience of two wars, the one redeeming feature of such conflict is the nobility it brings forth – the heroism, the endurance, and that quick sense of comradeship which springs up suddenly between the humble and the great. The first world war called out these qualities in full measure; and they were not lacking among the members and staff of the Association.

At the very outset Fanum House was faced with difficult problems. On the declaration of war a good many members had their cars detained abroad, and these had to be brought back. Then many questions arose. Would there be a petrol shortage? Would cars be commandeered? Would there be lighting restrictions? Would the speed limit operate in an emergency? And (as more and more of the Fanum members and staff of military age went off to fight) how was the organisation to be kept alive?

At first no one knew the answers to these questions: but still the Association acted promptly. Within a few hours every member was asked by circular whether he was prepared to place his car or motor cycle at the disposal of the government. A few weeks later, when 20,000 motorists had sent back favourable replies, a list was prepared against the day when government departments would notify the Association of their needs.

Soon members' cars were in demand to convey wounded soldiers to hospital or to take army recruits to their depots. In South Wales they played their part when batches of penniless refugees from Belgium arrived at Cardiff station. But perhaps the most striking of these varied schemes followed a War Office query one Saturday morning asking whether, in a certain eventuality, the A A could transport several hundred troops at emergency speed from an inland town to a north-east seaport. At once instructions to help muster the cars were passed from patrol to patrol on all the roads leading from London to the north, and Stenson Cooke himself dashed up to York to consult with military staff officers on operational details. Thus, by the Monday morning, 300 motor cars and motor cycles were occupying the Doncaster racecourse, a huge marquee had been erected for the drivers' messing and sleeping, and the correct drill for moving off when required had been worked out to the last minute and the last man. The cavalcade was not required in the end; but its lessons were.

The Association had meanwhile been changing shape as its staff diminished – and changing rapidly. From the start Stenson Cooke (an old volunteer officer himself) had kindled such a flame of patriotic enthusiasm that some 500 staff members voluntarily joined up for service. Many of these were enlisted in the 8th (Cyclist) Battalion of the Essex Regiment, in which the Secretary himself was given a commission. It was characteristic that he lost no time in letting the world know of the AA's contribution to the war effort, for on the day his first 100 patrols entrained for Colchester depot on their way to active service he had them photographed together and then marched them through the streets so that London might see his fit and well disciplined patrols *en masse* for the first time.

Stenson Cooke took care also to let the public know that no patrolmen were being retained on the roads if they were eligible for military service, though this soon became obvious. Members not only began to notice a number of one armed and one eyed patrols (who did surprisingly well in their unaccustomed jobs) but also discovered that some of the roadside telephone boxes had been closed up. It therefore seemed a little bizarre that this patriotic economy should have been accompanied by an eruption of police traps – including one in the Bagshot district where, to everyone's delight, the first eight cars to be trapped one day were labelled 'OHMS'.

In the early days of 1915 the Automobile Association was approaching the 100,000 mark. Its war activities had been so widely extended

that Lord Kitchener acknowledged them in a public tribute at Guild-
hall, but the normal work had to continue even with such a depleted
staff. Thus, in January, patrols were hard at work in the Thames valley where roads were under water and garages and other buildings
inundated by abnormal floods. Two months later the Metropolitan
Police invited the A A to warn its members that prosecution would be
continuous and severe if there was any further flouting of the regulations forbidding the use of powerful headlights. The Association had
hitherto been defending members on headlight charges although,
strictly speaking, the free legal defence scheme applied solely to
offences under the 1903 *Motor Car Act*. This privilege was now withdrawn, and at the same time patrols were stationed on main roads at
the boundaries of the metropolitan area to give headlight warnings.

In these and many other ways the old tradition of service was carried on, and not only in this country. Early in the war the committee
decided to make a gift of 100 motor ambulances to the hard pressed
French army. The first ten vehicles were in fact sent over to France
within a few weeks of the appeal, and on 12th February 1915 the next
fifty were lined up along The Mall for review by King George V. On
the French side of the Channel, President Poincaré reviewed the rest
of the ambulances when they arrived in Paris during the last week of
July, and a number were then sent to Belgium.

For the Allies 1916–17 was a period of great stress and strain,
and – like every other national institution – the Association was affected by the events of the time. Its membership declined. There were
further lighting restrictions. Motor taxation was increased, and there
was a sad deterioration in road surfaces. At the same time the Association was maintaining its own special war activities. Thus, every
night, a squad of the A A section of the special constabulary appeared
on duty with machines lined up and ready for such emergency calls as
the zeppelin raids on London.

During the grim twelve months of 1917 motoring was one of the
nation's forbidden pastimes, if only because the sale of petrol was

restricted. But the A A still had work to do – and not least over that
problem of petrol supply which always causes trouble in wartime. It
appeared in March that private owners (whose cars were being com-
pulsorily laid up and would therefore be on the roads for only a fraction of the year) would be expected to pay their motor licence fee for
the whole twelve months. At once the grievance was taken up with
the Chancellor of the Exchequer, who as quickly acknowledged the
injustice and promised a remedy. But meanwhile there were many
people who wondered if petrol would continue to be scarce after the
war – and, if it were, whether an alternative fuel could not be found.

Now petrol was the very lifeblood of the AA. Hence, early in
1918 (by which time its membership had dropped below 50,000), the
Association offered a prize of £1,000 for the best invention by which
coal gas could be used as a fuel for motor cars and motor cycles. The
conditions were that motorists should be able to carry sufficient gas in
a small space to provide the equivalent of several gallons of petrol;
that the weight should not exceed 140 lb; and that the cost to the
motorist should not exceed £20 or an annual hiring charge of £5.

Unfortunately, this competition proved abortive. A stream of
specifications flowed in, but only eleven inventors seemed to satisfy
the conditions. And these, when invited to forward their devices,
seemed curiously reluctant to do so.

It was all very disappointing, especially as petrol was the major
theme of the year. At the annual meeting in July, Joynson-Hicks could
hail the fact that the Association had more than £145,000 in hand for
reconstruction and propaganda after the war; it was intended, for example, to double the number of patrols. But petrol rather than patrols
was soon his dominant topic. One company, he declared, had already
stated that it had 80,000,000 gallons of spirit stored in various tanks
throughout the world, waiting to come to Britain when the war was
over. But, in the first five months of 1918, more gallons – '6,000,000
surplus gallons', 'Jix' called them – were imported than during the
corresponding period of the previous year. 'I think,' he added, 'that

E

as motorists the Automobile Association is entitled to ask our friends
of the services to do everything possible to avoid waste of petrol.'

One might have thought that such matters would have been forgotten when, a few months later, the war ended and the nation gave
itself up to rejoicing. In London, certainly, there were tumultuous
scenes which have become legendary; and for at least two days the
human tides of celebration swirled in and out of Leicester Square and
around the walls of Fanum House. But the committee simply closed
its windows against the noise and got down to the work in hand.

Among the many things which the 1914 war ended was the bulk of that prejudice against the motor car which had inflamed so many in the pre-war years. Henceforth, as the demand for small cars increased, motorists ceased to be 'fur clad murderers', 'goggled assassins', or even 'shrieking stink pots'. The times had changed.

So also, in a sense, had the Automobile Association. Many of its problems were as old as itself, but others were new and challenging. During the war the Association's assets had leaped up to more than £250,000 because, despite the skeleton nature of the wartime organisation, many members had kept up their subscriptions. The membership, on the other hand, had dwindled from nearly 100,000 when war broke out to about 36,000 at the armistice. But this was not a matter for anxiety. No sooner was the war over than there was a rush of new members and of old members asking to be re-elected.

The Association's first problem was still the vital one of petrol: and here it acted with speed. The moment the war ended the A A urged the government to modify its restrictions, and this was done in a limited degree. Unfortunately the price of imported petrol rose steeply, and there were complaints when motorists found that a gallon of the spirit which cost 1s 9d before the war now cost some 4s.

On this vexed question the Association had strong views; for most of the fuel was combine-produced abroad whereas at home there was benzole, a cheaper British-produced spirit which the A A engineers thought should be more widely patronised. In furtherance of its 1919 campaign for benzole the Association urged its members to store this spirit in gardens and outhouses, and had fifty-gallon drums specially made for members to hire at 10s a year. By autumn it had organised a 10,000 mile road test of benzole, using a Sunbeam car whose average

mileage per gallon worked out at 24.57. However, even this enterprise – backed up a few months later by an impressive petition urging
the government to create independent sources of fuel supply – had to
take second place to a scheme that was destined to revolutionise
the motorist's life.

In the winter of 1919-20, at Aldermaston near Newbury, the
Association erected the first pump filling station in the history of
British motoring. That it was erected at all was due to a sudden
awareness that distribution of petrol in two-gallon tins was wasteful
and costly, and to the A A's wish to popularise benzole. It was a simple scheme, but one so effective that by the midsummer of 1921 there
were eight stations, the petrol companies were resolved to set up
their own, and the A A was retiring from the busy scene it had created.

Abroad, meantime, the countries of the continent had begun to
bristle with new import duties on cars. In France, for instance, the
duty was raised to seventy per cent – which meant that the less
wealthy man who dreamed of Chartres or Carcassonne was likely to
go no farther than Clacton pier. But the Association came to his
rescue. If he could provide a guarantee from his bank, the A A under-
took to be responsible for the duty.

At home these early post-war years were soon productive. For
some time to come most of the patrols were still to be cycle borne,
but the cheerful chug of the patrolman's motor cycle began to be
heard on the roads, and gradually the sidecar outfit also became
familiar. The object of this new service was to help members whose
cars had broken down to make repairs if possible and – if the breakdown was serious and no telephone was handy – to drive to the nearest A A agent and thus get help. At the same time many of the telephone boxes were illuminated at night, and new officials were appointed to supervise certain services in those administrative areas
which the Association defined soon after the armistice.

Here too, of course, we see fulfilment of the now deeply engrained
idea of service: and in return membership climbed steeply. Having at

last attained the first 100,000 on 6th February 1920, the Association rose to 150,000 strong by October. Such a rise was startling, but it was probably due not only to the expanding road services but to the Association's long campaign to secure better conditions for motorists through Parliament. In the main this battle was waged through the Motor Legislation Committee, a body set up by the A A and the Society of Motor Manufacturers and Traders to challenge unfair official discrimination against motorists.

On taxation in particular the Association took a strong line: but this it had done ever since Lloyd George in 1909 introduced a graduated scale of horse power taxation along with a petrol tax of 3d a gallon. During the war this levy had been increased; but now, as from New Year's Day 1921, a tax of £1 per horse power on private cars was substituted for the earlier scale and the petrol tax was abolished. The A A opposed this arrangement on the ground that motorists should be taxed on fuel consumption rather than on horse power: in other words, those who used the roads most should pay the most money. As one member said of horse power taxation at the annual meeting, 'It would be just as sensible to tax the teapot or the cigarette box, irrespective of how much tea was made or how many cigarettes were smoked'. Besides, it looked as if motorists, who were now paying vast sums in taxation (supposedly to improve the roads), were to carry burdens from which other road users were exempt.

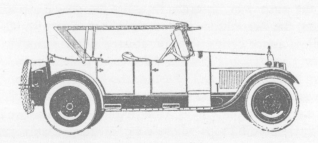

The record of the next few years is one of steady progress, due to a
change of outlook less perhaps by the Association than by the authorities. But in its leadership there had reluctantly to be a change. In
particular the legal brain and business experience of Sir William
Joynson-Hicks must have been greatly missed when he joined the
government as a junior minister on his way to the cabinet and so had
to resign from the Chairmanship after sixteen years' service. The new
Chairman – for twelve months – was that old pioneer Charles Jarrott.
The vice-chairmen were Walter Gibbons (who had recently been
knighted) and Charles McWhirter, who was elected Chairman in
1923 and continued as such until his death in the second world war.
But here, with the A A under new helmsmen, we must pick out some
of the beacons of the time.

In 1924 (when membership reached 200,000) it is interesting to
note a stronger insistence on road safety, for the handbooks of the
time are spattered with road advice to members. And certainly the
Automobile Association's constant, and still continuing, efforts to improve road manners enhanced its own relations with the authorities,
and eased many situations which might otherwise have remained
somewhat difficult.

Early the same year, in order to assist the growing traffic in the
dark hours, the Association started a night road service which soon
made yellow motor cycles with illuminated sidecars familiar. As the
Manchester Guardian put it when these experimental patrols became
permanent in Lancashire and Cheshire the following year: 'Nothing
is more remarkable than the skeleton of roads on which the Association has daily and nightly eyes. One might add ears as well, for on
those great remote hilltops whose conquest may often mean break-

down to the motorist, there are telephones under a lighted double A, bespeaking relief in distress'.

A year later still, in July 1926, the annual meeting of members was held under the slowly dispersing shadows of the general strike. Though there were many reasons why that unhappy affair had collapsed so quickly at the beginning of June, the main reason was probably the resolve of the majority of people not to be deprived of their essential services. To this end the existence of 1,300,000 privately owned motor vehicles was naturally all-important, since most of them came to the rescue when the engine drivers left their footplates and the buses and lorries stopped running.

From the beginning it was evident that the AA – which now had more than 275,000 members – would be required to play some part. It was also likely to be accused of strike breaking. But on this count it is noteworthy that the committee, with a natural reluctance to be embroiled in party politics, made no formal appeal for volunteers. The real impetus came from the members themselves, who immediately and spontaneously inundated headquarters with offers to put their cars at the government's disposal. Inevitably, therefore, the Association's offices all over the country were kept open day and night to enrol these volunteers and to provide cars for both official and unofficial purposes. The road patrol system also was soon busily controlling traffic, giving mechanical assistance to non-members as well as members, and letting telephone boxes be freely used for the control of vital transport movements. Dispatch riders were provided and special AA vehicles carried official messages about the country. Soldiers on leave, police officers, telephone operators and hospital nurses were taken back to duty. Cars were mobilised to distribute the government's newspaper, *The British Gazette*, and to carry mails. It was a tragic and troubled time; but fortunately it was soon past and at the annual meeting a few weeks later it could be claimed that membership had topped 300,000, that the road staff during the year had covered more than 18,000,000 miles, and that the touring department

had issued routes whose mileage was equal to 5,000 times the length
of the equator. Finally, it was in 1926 that the Association completed
its move into the eight storey building by Leicester Square which
stands in all its spaciousness today as Fanum House, London.

This move was timely, for the growth of membership suddenly
became phenomenal. In April 1927 no fewer than 11,120 new members were elected at the monthly committee meeting – and this
record figure, when published, merely encouraged a further torrent of
applications. That these striking proofs of confidence should have
coincided with the Association's renewed campaign against the system
of motor vehicle taxation was probably significant. For this was an
issue on which the AA – with its traditional concern for the small
man as well as the big one – was always consistent. Certainly in 1927
it had strong support, not only for its criticism of horse power taxation but on another vital tax issue. At the beginning of July patrols
carried a petition to Parliament, signed by more than 360,000 motorists, protesting strongly against £12,000,000 of motor taxation
revenue being diverted from road building by a government raid on
the Road Fund.

In the meantime the bread and butter work went steadily on – and
not least in Ireland, where the Association was completing its task of
signposting all Irish main roads and opening its first two roadside
telephone boxes. The scheme had involved a great deal of hard and
intricate work, while the AA planned with county surveyors the
exact location of each sign, the directions and mileage it was to show,
and the fittings it would require. The agreement was that the AA
would supply the signs and fittings and that the county surveyors
would put them up.

Among those in the know there was some excitement because
officials in the six counties knew that 'the boys in the south' had had
their signs delivered a few weeks before but still hoped to get their
own up first. Then at last there came the great day when the Belfast
office heard that the Ulster signs were on their way from London.

PLATE 7 *The lady does not care what goes on in the engine. The lady may even have
forgotten to fill the tank. But her car has stopped in a convenient spot, and there is
somebody else to do the worrying.*

*Early in the history of motoring
the fair sex took to the roads.
Some of their fashions
were more practical than elegant:
others were decoratively inspired by the
coming of the automobile age.*

PLATE 8

PLATE 9

*The architecture
of ladies' millinery
was no stranger than
the architecture
of many pre-1914 cars.*

Soon a race was in progress; but Irish races, except between horses, can sometimes be leisurely affairs. For instance, in one county there had been such absolute silence that even headquarters letters remained unanswered. Eventually the local secretary wrote to fix an appointment with the county surveyor, some ninety miles away; but still getting no reply, he motored to the county town and made for the surveyor's office. To his disappointment he was told: 'Himself is out. He's round about the county. But if it's the signs you're after, well sure old Pat in the store beyont will be knowing all about them'. A visit to the store confirmed this. For there was Pat, seemingly at leisure and only too willing to pass the time of day.

'Well,' he said to the local secretary, 'I'm not rightly sure when himself does be going to put up the signs. It'll all depend on how he's fixed for the next week or so. I'll give him your message.' He then pointed at the stacks of gleaming signs. 'He'll hardly be likely to have them there foreby the spring. But you know,' he finally added, 'I can't help wondering why you're fashing yourself about these signs anyway. Sure, *I* know me way round this county blindfold.'

LATE 10 *The patrol, with all his technical knowledge and wide experience,*
may still find traditional methods best when dealing with an old fashioned puncture.

The year 1928 looked as if it would be an ordinary one of routine work, until in May the Association issued its famous promise to organise future travel by air as it had in the past organised road travel. This was not new in A A history. Back in 1909 the committee had established an aviation section – the Aerial Association, as it was sometimes called. But this had been disrupted by the 1914 war, so the immediate effect of this apparently new development was one of some surprise. Many newspapers made it front page news, and most of them seemed to think that just as the A A had made life on the roads more comfortable, so too its promised route maps, research and advice would revolutionise private flying. If the air tourist wished for weather reports, he would get them just as the motorist did. Air patrolmen, recruited from ex-members of the Royal Air Force, would be on duty at airfields. There was to be efficient aerial signposting – including the painting of place names in large letters on roofs of suitable buildings or emergency landing grounds – and propaganda to ensure that high chimneys, radio masts and other obstructions were provided with warning lights in the dark hours.

In the light of these advances the aviation department expanded so rapidly that only a year later, when the Schneider Trophy race took place over the Solent, the Association was able to provide air scouts on the adjacent landing fields to assist the hundreds of visiting pilots from all over Europe. By this time also maps and information, for home as well as for European use, were being supplied to pilot members. Soon the department was issuing international travel permits. And in 1930 it successfully defended its first aviation summons in circumstances which recalled the old Edwardian days when unduly pedantic policemen had drivers summoned because the letters and figures on their car registration plates were partly obscured by mud.

A pilot, flying from London to Derby, had landed in a small field and been asked by a policeman for his pilot's licence. This was duly produced. Later in the day the policeman reappeared with a new demand for the machine's certificate of airworthiness, which unfortunately the pilot had left behind at Heston. Faithfully on returning south he fulfilled his promise to forward the particulars of his certificate to the Derby police, and put the matter out of his mind. The Derby police on the other hand kept it in theirs; and some days later the pilot, having received a summons to appear on a charge of 'failing to produce the certificate of airworthiness when called upon to do so by a police constable', wisely put the affair in the hands of the Automobile Association and soon had the case dismissed.

A year later still (and until 1933, when the Air Ministry took the station over) the Association was transmitting continuous radio weather reports from Heston airfield for the benefit of private pilots. It also aided those pioneers whose historic flights straddled the world in the thirties – the Mollisons, for example – by planning their routes and collecting the latest information about weather conditions, the state of landing fields and foreign air regulations. None the less, for every one of these dramatic exploits the Association made arrangements for at least a hundred ordinary touring flights till all such pleasures were interrupted by the second world war.

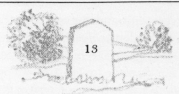

For the rest, the thirties opened for the AA on the controversial note created by the 1930 *Road Traffic Act*. When first published as a Bill this measure had been criticised on several counts; and although its amended form met some of the criticisms, there still seemed a likelihood that certain of the Association's worst fears were about to be realised. Yet some of the gains were substantial: the speed limit for private motor vehicles was abolished (this for years had been in the forefront of AA policy); driving tests for people suffering from physical disability were introduced (this also was AA policy); a highway code was authorised; and third party insurance was made compulsory for the first time.

On this last provision there was so much confusion that the Association had to warn its members that after 1st January 1930 motorists or motor cyclists would be unable to run their vehicles unless they produced an insurance certificate. But the insurance problem went further. A number of motorists who had failed to renew their licences had them suspended for twelve months. This alone was vexatious, for in many cases the failure to renew was only due to an oversight and no breach of the law was intended. But the trouble went even further than that. Did insurance apply to a motorist whose licence was out of date? To provide a valid answer to this vital question the Association consulted a leading KC, who gave his opinion that in the event of a third party claim the insurance company need not pay if the motorist lacked a proper licence. In effect the insurance companies decided to pay when the member's failure was due to simple oversight or to condonable circumstances such as absence abroad.

Proceedings in court under the Act brought another thorny crop of problems. For although in the old days motorists had become inured

to court proceedings on a single charge, they were now beset by multiple summonses arising from one incident. Thus, when the motorist
or his advocate entered court he did not know on which of perhaps
five charges the police would choose to proceed, since the summons
could be for driving recklessly, in a manner dangerous to the public,
at a speed dangerous to the public, without due care and attention, or
without reasonable consideration for other people using the road. It
seemed an unfair procedure, and the AA made spirited protests.

In the meantime shoals of private complaints were pouring in to
Fanum House, and the motorist's mood was made no more temperate
by the fact that these multiple charge cases and the Association's protests coincided with bitter weather and appalling road conditions. All
over the country patrols on special night duty were acting as pilots to
motorists who had found the fog impenetrable, lighting flares at road
junctions, sprinkling ice-bound patches with sand long after roadmen
had left their posts, and giving headquarters the latest reports on road
conditions. However, the battle over the multiple summonses was to
continue long after the fog had cleared and the ice had melted; and
though the Association was not to win outright, at least this particularly exasperating form of charge became less frequent.

During all these unavoidable differences with authority the services continued to grow. Membership was soon well over 400,000.
There were more than 400 roadside telephone boxes, and the Association was spending some £500,000 a year on its road service alone.
By this time, of course, the patrols had long been familiar and popular
figures on the highway, yet never before had their versatility been so
often remarked on. Some of the unexpected tasks which came their
way are described later in this book, but since their courtesy and
efficiency were among the chief reasons for the Association's growth
in the thirties some notable deeds should be recorded here. There was
one single day in the summer of 1931, for instance, when these
knights of the road (as they were so often called in the press) captured a dangerous lunatic and brought him back to the mental home

from which he had escaped; saved from destruction four cars which
had caught fire; brought two runaway horses to a standstill; had two
alleged car thieves arrested as a result of information supplied to the
police; and rescued a drowning boy from the river Wye.

The next three years passed quickly. They were, in the main, years
of consolidation, which is seldom an exciting process. New branches
were opened and new publications issued. Foreign touring facilities
were extended to at least a dozen new countries. And so large was the
membership that at the 1932 distribution the Post Office had to handle
180 tons of handbooks. Incidentally, it was also in 1932 that members
were menaced by an outbreak of motor banditry and the whole road
patrol system was brought to an even brisker alert than usual. In a
simpler setting, the roadside telephone boxes were thoughtfully provided with drinking troughs for dogs. Night service vans began to
operate on arterial roads with heavy traffic. And a new road safety
campaign was started.

In return, public esteem was not withheld. In 1933 Stenson Cooke
was knighted – to the delight of both the committee and the staff.
Again, no sooner was that agreeable ceremony over than the Association, on 24th August, enrolled its 500,000th member, and Sir
Stenson could reflect with pride how twenty-eight years earlier the
A A's capital was less than £100, whereas its annual revenue in the
year of his knighthood was £1,000,000 and still rising.

It has been said before that, if Christmas usually brought warming
news, a chill wind came with the New Year; and at first it looked as
if the New Year of 1935 was to be no exception. For certain mis-
chievous people now developed a mania for stealing fire extinguishers
from the roadside telephone boxes, and considerable vigilance had to
be exercised before the epidemic could be arrested. Happily, this
was more than offset by a New Year's Day reduction of twenty-five
per cent in the horse power taxation of private cars and motor cycles.
There was also the spring decision of the railway companies to let the
A A fix three red and three white reflectors on the gates at level

crossings; but it was the important horse power tax relief which caused the greatest pleasure and notably stimulated the production and ownership of motor vehicles, especially the smaller ones. Here also the AA could claim some of the credit, since never at any time had it relaxed its efforts to put motor taxation squarely on petrol rather than on engine capacity – or, if this were refused, to have the horse power tax materially reduced. Legitimately, therefore, Charles McWhirter as Chairman could claim a good share of the credit for this advance when the Association met for its annual meeting.

At this half way house of the thirties he had other good things to tell, and one was most reassuring. In the previous year Mr Hore-Belisha's new *Traffic Act* had introduced a thirty miles per hour speed limit in built up areas, and instituted driving tests. Unfortunately there was some danger that innocent offenders against the speed limit might be unnecessarily prosecuted, and every case was vigorously contested where the member's defence seemed reasonable. The effect was remarkable: nearly half the speed limit cases brought by the police were either dismissed or leniently dealt with. And this was only one of the offences against which members had to be defended. All in all, McWhirter could point to the striking fact that during the previous twelve months 6,000 cases brought by the police had been dismissed through the Association's efforts.

It seemed natural, therefore, that in May 1936 the AA should have recruited its 600,000th member. Thus encouraged, it added a few more refinements to its various services, the first of which again concerned the law. Ever since its introduction of free legal defence before the first world war, the Association had omitted manslaughter from the charges on which it was prepared to defend its members. But the position had changed. Between 1933 and 1935, of 364 drivers charged with manslaughter 267 were acquitted; and this naturally made the Association think again. In the majority of these cases the defendants had in fact been proved innocent – at great cost to themselves – and there seemed once again an excessive zeal, when accidents occurred, for the police to assume that the motorist rather than the pedestrian had been at fault. At this point Fanum House decided to extend free legal defence to manslaughter cases, though reserving the right to refuse assistance where the charge was obviously well founded.

But here we must glance more closely at these legal imbroglios, since the middle and late thirties – with their great efflux of cars on to the roads and far reaching Traffic Acts to govern their movements – confronted the Automobile Association once again with problems reminiscent of that battle of the roads which had called it into being. The thirty miles per hour speed limit in built up areas was the biggest thorn in its side; and there can be little doubt that some authorities were excessively zealous, for the AA in the twelve months preceding July 1936 secured 7,400 dismissals of cases brought against its members. It is hardly surprising that in October the AA issued a statement condemning the number of prosecutions for trivial road offences, especially when brought on the evidence of a single policeman.

In 1937 (and by now the statement occasions no surprise) the membership continued to rise and the services to expand. Members in fact used the services so freely that in the very first month of the year they posted 155,400 letters to Fanum House in London, and there must have been an equivalent number in the area offices. Yet this was January, which was far from being a peak month like July or August. (Incidentally, for those who live on statistics, there were now 11,000 members named Smith, 7,000 named Jones and 6,000 who answered to Brown. More surprising perhaps was the embellishment of the members' roll by 200 people whose name began with Z.)

But, whatever their names, members had food for thought when they read in the newspapers that each male member of the staff was being offered, in addition to his annual holiday, fourteen days' special leave (also with full pay) provided it was devoted to training for an essential service in the event of a national emergency. Widely noticed and commended, this seed became a sturdy plant the following spring when the War Office decided to recruit a supplementary reserve of the

PLATE 11 *To almost anywhere where motorists may congregate – even to a sp normally so quiet as Portland Bill – the AA carries a wide range of servic through its mobile office*

*Varied activities
fell to the A A during
the first world war.*

PLATE 12

Corps of Military Police from the patrol staff of the A A. Leading up
to this decision was not only the general need for traffic control in an
increasingly mechanised army, but what the War Office called the
'unqualified success' of the forty patrols who had acted as military
police on traffic duties during the army's manoeuvres the previous
year. The appeal was remarkably successful, too, since 500 men were
wanted and within two or three days 900 applied.

What happened to these volunteers we shall see only too soon, for
the war shadows across Europe were darkening quickly in the winter
of 1938 and the spring and summer of 1939. It seemed, indeed, a
strange irony of fate that, with almost three-quarters of a million
members on its books just before war broke out, the A A's strength
and prospects should have seemed so bright when the future for the
world appeared so sombre.

F

When war broke out on 3rd September 1939 the Automobile Association was faced with some of the most complicated problems in its
history. That it would have a part to play in the struggle was obvious.
But first the interests of its members touring the continent had to be
safeguarded, and this was no light task. Indeed, so many cars were
making for the Channel ports towards the end of August that the
port officers had to work at least eighteen hours a day to get them
safely on board the ships; and on one memorable day they even
disembarked 700 cars with the A A badge at a single port.

But this was only one of many emergency problems. Within a few
days the staff was drastically reduced as its members went to the
services. Then, without interrupting the normal service to members,
the chief departments at Fanum House, London, were transferred to
Guildford, leaving an emergency headquarters behind to carry on in
the old sandbagged building. In preparation for the evacuation of
London (how oddly that reads now!) the Association had also spent
many months in preparing signs for the whole of London's one way
evacuation routes and in making sure that, given a minute's notice,
all could be erected within a few hours.

The inevitable bugbear of petrol rationing was also swift to appear,
and with it the usual complications. Many members complained of
hardships and inequalities, and finally the Association suggested to
the government that appeal tribunals should be set up to consider
them in detail. As for the A A's own fuel consumption, until it was
known whether any petrol at all would be allowed for the patrols they
were instructed to cover their beats by pedal cycle, a number of staff
cars and vans were dispensed with, and 850 road service outfits were
laid up for the duration of the war.

To make matters worse the police in certain areas suddenly renewed their old-time prosecutions against motorists for speeding and
other offences, and the fines inflicted at different courts varied from
10s to as much as £20 for going, say, at twenty-three miles an hour
in the blackout instead of at the new speed limit of twenty. On this the
Association issued a spirited statement of protest. It is true that the
blackout increased the death rate on the roads alarmingly, but the
Association felt that technical prosecutions with such arbitrary punish-
ments were far from helpful.

It was thus hardly surprising that for some time to come the legal
defence department had to defend a great many motorists charged
with lighting offences, which it did with some success. There was
certainly one notable victory when a motorist was acquitted because
the advocate proved that, although the headlamp in question did not
conform to the original regulations, it did comply with an alternative
method of screening subsequently approved by the Ministry of Home
Security. Nor did it go unnoticed in this case that a police constable
under cross examination explained that a quarter of a mile equalled
forty or fifty yards – a calculation which prompted the magistrate to
remark that the constable would have no difficulty in winning the
police open quarter-mile.

While these and many other problems were piling up, the 800
officers and patrols of the A A in the Corps of Royal Military Police
won praise for their share in the swift movement of the British Ex-
peditionary Force in France in the first few weeks of the war. For
such a task the patrols were highly qualified. Not only did they have
experience of directing traffic and giving mechanical aid when necessary, but they were also expert in signposting; and this in the movement of armies is a vital requirement, especially in strange countries.

But tragically soon the red caps were in retreat as the Germans
forced the BEF back to the beaches of Dunkirk in the early summer
of 1940 and the historic evacuation began. Soon too there were con-
sultations between the Association and the staff of the Commander-

in-Chief, Home Forces, on the best use of the remaining road staff in
the event of invasion. The telephone boxes, naturally, were to be
placed unreservedly at the disposal of the military. At the same time
the 100,000 AA signposts which had taken so many years to erect
were obliterated or torn down; every kind of publication which
might help the enemy was virtually suspended; and every application
for a route was carefully scrutinised. There were many other plans
under review when suddenly in the late summer there came the horror
of the blitz. But here – in its great test of endurance – we might well
let the Association speak for itself.

'One of the worst nights,' says a record of the time, 'was when two
large bombs descended on our island site within a few feet of the
Leicester Square frontage. Two buildings were entirely demolished;
others next to us rendered uninhabitable. Most of Fanum's windows
were blown out, partitions thrown around and many doors deranged.
Splinters and glass were everywhere. Some of our papers were found
two streets away and returned. A cold east wind whistled through the
building: there was neither heat, telephone, gas nor water. The staff
turned up its coat collars, huddled close and carried on doggedly with
the stream of emergency calls that had become routine. Hurricane
lamps, candles and torches were brought into use in the blackout and
the work went on in an atmosphere charged with the fumes of
smouldering, sodden fabrics. At night the basement housed numbers
of women clerks from government departments, many dozing on hard
wooden chairs.'

Despite such trials the staff were not deflected from their duty.
They had to deal, for instance, with a new scheme of heavier motor
taxation at the beginning of 1940, with the likelihood of still more
stringent petrol rationing, and with the transport dislocations caused
by enemy bombs. There was also a 'Help Your Neighbour' plan
which gave motorists living within twenty miles of Charing Cross
extra petrol coupons if they pledged themselves to carry passengers
to and from their homes and businesses for a distance not exceeding

twenty miles a day. The pledges were signed and the coupons issued at the headquarters of the motoring organisations, and queues besieged the AA office at the end of October when the scheme began.

In the meantime, membership during the first eighteen months of the war had declined by more than 239,000. If that was only to be expected as more and more cars were sold or laid up for the duration, members with cars engaged on essential duties and the patrols still left on the roads certainly did not expect those fierce blizzards which in the New Year of 1941 – the worst for a quarter of a century – tested their skill and endurance to the uttermost. In some drifts, ten feet deep, cars were buried for at least a week. Near Preston a hearse with a coffin was snowed up for five days on the way to a burial. But, in fact, all kinds of vehicles were involved in a vast traffic hold-up which the police and the AA patrols together did their best to disentangle in the bitterest weather conditions most of them could remember.

For the rest of the war the Association continued to grapple with difficulties which are still fresh in memory, though it did so after 1942 without the services of Sir Stenson Cooke, who died on 19th November at the age of sixty-eight. Among his colleagues there was a deep sense of loss not only because his genius for organisation was so marked and his personal qualities so endearing, but because he had stood for so long as a symbol of the Association's colourful history.

By good fortune there was no loss of tradition or continuity under the new Secretary, Edward Fryer, or under Charles McWhirter's successor as Chairman, the Rev Canon F. W. Hassard-Short. The tall silver haired canon had been a trusted friend of the motoring community since the early years of the century, when he first helped to found the Cardiff Motor Club and later became a member of the Motor Union's committee. Later still his election to the committee of the AA and MU, when these two bodies amalgamated in 1910, gave him fresh opportunities to display his wisdom in counsel and his gift for reducing complicated issues to a simple form. Edward Fryer's talents and experience were no less valued. He too had been a motor-

ist almost from the start of the century. Then for a time he held a post
with the Motor Union and became the first midland manager of the
AA after the fusion. Having also served the Association faithfully as
deputy secretary for many years he thus had all its problems at his
finger tips, and was only unlucky in taking over at a time of such disturbance. Happily, like Stenson Cooke before him, he was able to
keep the organisation in being though the heavens fell.

For difficulties now multiplied. The end of even the basic petrol
ration in 1942 was to cause a further sharp decline in membership,
and many of the popular peacetime services became a thing of the
past. The already emaciated patrol service shrank to a skeleton,
though the few patrols left on the roads – with their tin hats, respira-
tors, first aid equipment and fire extinguishers – had many vital
functions to perform, and one patrol in 1943 even tracked down a
German officer escaped from a prisoner of war camp. A great deal of
information, including special signs, had to be provided for the
American military authorities when they arrived in this country. And
the home touring department, looking rather elderly by this time,
provided millions of miles of routes for our own service and civil
authorities. When one remembers that the staff was only a fraction of
the pre-war establishment it is clear that it did not waste its time. Nor
did the rest of the nation; and in consequence many great institutions
began to see victory in sight by the end of 1943 and turned to the
problems of peace without any slackening of war endeavours.

Among these were the motoring organisations, who foresaw that
acute road problems would arise. They knew, for one thing, that
since motoring for pleasure's sake had become as rare as ostriches
in Oswaldtwistle road development had been seriously curbed. They
believed also that there would be a struggle to get the wartime road
restrictions removed, since bureaucratic clamps imposed in an emergency are seldom easy to get rid of when the emergency is over.

Faced, therefore, with too many uncertainties for comfort, the
Automobile Association, the Royal Automobile Club and the Royal

Scottish Automobile Club decided to act in concert on political matters and formed a Standing Joint Committee. This body, which met for the first time on 24th January 1944, at once became a useful piece of machinery, which ministers of the Crown regarded with the greater respect because it removed the complaint that motoring spokesmen gave conflicting advice on road questions. But its main achievements were to be reserved for the un-piping days of peace.

When the war ended in 1945 the A A was plunged into a long conflict over the issues of petrol and motor taxation. Besides this, the Standing Joint Committee had started a campaign for road development and safety which still goes on. But it was fuel which caused the greatest disturbance in those years. At the end of the war, the Minister of Fuel and Power gave motorists a small basic petrol ration. A year later the pressure to abolish rationing was very strong, since both the motoring bodies and the motor trade claimed that ample supplies existed inside the sterling area. A year later still, during an economic crisis, the government withdrew the basic ration at the expense of a storm which made the Standing Joint Committee protest to the Prime Minister that the hardships imposed by this new essay in austerity would be out of all proportion to the savings effected. At the same time a national petition signed by a million motorists was carried to Parliament by patrolmen, and a second million soon followed afterwards.

This was all hardly surprising, since by this time motorists were genuinely resentful. In 1947 they were paying almost £94,000,000 in motor taxation of all kinds, and the new road construction which this sum was supposed to finance seemed to be at a standstill. Moreover, petrol rationing was at an end in many European countries. So it was little wonder that, while motorists' resentment was deepening into anger, the A A grew at a phenomenal rate. Fortunately for everyone, however, on 26th May 1950 petrol rationing ceased after more than ten years, and motorists began to drive up to filling stations with a new sense of freedom.

But always there seemed to be imps of mischief behind the motor's driving force. To look ahead, when petrol workers struck in the autumn of 1953 the pumps in the London garages were soon running so dry that the telephone lines leading into Fanum House were over-run by calls from members who had themselves run out of fuel or were about to do so. Quite often the Association came to the rescue, but when the worst happened arrangements were made to tow stranded vehicles off the roads and give them shelter. Then also, when it became clear that no more petrol would be delivered in London, a survey was made of places where petrol was still available, so that a rationed quantity could be supplied to doctors and others whose work was essential. The A A's public relations experts meanwhile were issuing continuous bulletins to the press and the BBC so that motor-ists contemplating journeys should be warned if their destination lay in a 'dry zone'. In the end it was gratifying – since official sources were remarkably silent throughout the strike – that many members who had profited from these services sent Fanum House warm thanks for its initiative.

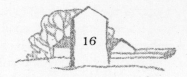

16

Though these petrol issues had been vexatious, the Association's constructive work meanwhile had been impelled by a vigorous new dynamic. To look back on the post-war period is, in fact, to see it as one of the most remarkably successful of the A A's five decades. In the days before the first world war there had been the first great phase when the Association gave to its members patrols, roadside telephone boxes, appointed hotels and garages, the first A A branch offices, facilities for easier home and foreign travel, road signs, free legal defence and many of the other services which have so long been familiar. Thereafter, between the wars, though undoubtedly there were new departures from time to time (the aviation department, for instance) the Association's main effort was concentrated on consolidating and improving these services and bringing to their enjoyment an ever increasing number of motorists. That this succeeded brilliantly we know. By the time the Hitler war broke out the Automobile Association was easily the largest motoring organisation in the world and its initial letters were almost as familiar as those of the British Broadcasting Corporation.

Inevitably, however, the war interrupted the long period of steady progress. Thus, by that maytime of 1945 when the guns ceased to fire in Europe, the Association's membership had dropped by some 400,000, while the patrols who numbered some 300 compared with 2,500 in peacetime were forced to wear battledress on the roads because their old-time uniforms were impossible to obtain. To any fainthearts at Fanum (if such there were) it must have seemed that the traditional concepts of service to members and *esprit de corps* among the staff were about to become mere catchwords rather than watchwords.

But the very reverse happened. While committee and staff were fighting for a fuller flow of petrol they were also launching a series of new plans which make the post-war years comparable with the adventuresome ones before the first world war. Let us put them, as it were, under a moving spotlight.

In 1946 our beam shines strongly on the start of the free breakdown service – a new departure for the A A, which enabled members to be reimbursed for expenses incurred when their cars broke down on the road. There was soon no doubt of this scheme's popularity or of its effect on a membership list which was growing again at a phenomenal rate. For this there were of course additional reasons – the fight for petrol, the Association's constant appeals to the authorities to turn blitzed sites into car parks, its widely noticed co-operation with the police on the great day of the Victory Parade (which alone meant the erection of 1,000 signs) and its introduction of mobile roadside offices to give members service and information during holiday seasons or during parades and sporting events. Yet the war was only a little more than a twelvemonth behind. The following year was to be more fruitful still.

During 1947, 500 new road service outfits came into service; £30,000 worth of claims was recovered for members without litigation; dismissals were secured in sixty per cent of the legal cases defended; and a new office was opened at Carlisle. Such progress, as we have now learned to expect, was reflected in an influx of new members so remarkable that by the end of 1947 the membership was 741,000, or 10,000 more than it had been before the war. Equally strikingly, it was to rise again very rapidly during the next twelve months, though on the surface 1948 seems to be less crowded with new schemes flowing from London or the area offices.

Yet that year was far from being uneventful. For if our travelling spotlight dims at the death of Edward Fryer, whose secretarial wisdom and foresight had been tested to the uttermost in difficult years, it lights again at the inevitable compensations for his loss. The new

Secretary, William V. Gibson, was yet another of those officials who had spent his life in the interest of motorists. Originally a Motor Union man, he came to the A A at the fusion and devoted himself to the new body's legal and parliamentary work until his appointment as an assistant secretary shortly before the war. That this faithful servant should have been appointed to the A A's highest executive post at a time of its most rapid expansion seems fitting, for motorists owed much to his long experience and genial wisdom.

But here, with Gibson settled in the secretarial chair at headquarters, we might well let our spotlight illumine some of the incessant activities of the Association in the countryside. There, judging by the committee's annual report, the traditional public service of the road staff was as brisk as ever. It is noted, for instance, that a patrol was able by his timely warning to save a Glasgow-London express train from almost certain disaster when the line was obstructed by heavy masonry dislodged from a bridge by a passing lorry. Again, in August, the patrols played their part when serious flooding in the Scottish border country disrupted communications over a wide area, put forty bridges out of use, broke up road surfaces and started a number of landslides. In response to urgent requests the A A rushed temporary signs to the stricken districts and rapidly marked out all the diversions, the blocked roads, and the stretches where only single line traffic was in force. In addition the patrol staff rendered yeoman service to the local inhabitants by helping to save livestock and salvage property.

Once again, then, the versatility of the patrols had been displayed. And indeed it was the very variety of their functions which prompted the A A, before the year was out, to open a school at Camden Town where patrols could be given intensive training in all the branches of their wide activity. Within three years the school was moved to Widmerpool in Nottinghamshire, where it was greatly expanded so that those who had for so long been the backbone of the A A could provide a still higher standard of service.

If 1948 had thus been a year of satisfactory progress, 1949 was even more promising. For a start there came an old wine in a new bottle, when at last the committee was able to republish that handbook which had been so long held up by the national shortage of paper. But also there were sparkling new wines to savour, of which the most important were the continental breakdown service abroad and the night breakdown service at home. Though inevitably on a smaller scale than its companion, the foreign scheme attracted early notice. For the government had relaxed its foreign currency restrictions a little, and by April (when the breakdown scheme was announced) more than 20,000 members going on holiday had asked the Association to speed the passage of their cars across the Channel and through the French customs. Many of these felt that major repairs to British motor cars at the time could seldom be carried out promptly by continental garages, and hence arose the Association's plan to bear the main cost of returning a damaged vehicle to the port from which the member had booked his return passage.

Yet if this scheme was an imaginative and useful adjunct to the services of the AA, the start of the night breakdown service was clearly a major road development. For the first time the newest techniques of radio communication were made available to members in trouble late at night, when many garages were closed. Furthermore, the success of the new scheme was to pave the way to 1952 and what became an ever growing system of radio road patrols in constant touch with AA offices and therefore more swiftly divertible than before to members telephoning for assistance. Not surprisingly, these new advances at once caught the motorist's imagination.

Since then the web of radio control for motorists has spread from the land to the narrow seas. It was only a year or so later that the now thoroughly radio minded Association turned its attention to the use of ship to shore radio in the Channel in order that port officers could give or receive advance information enabling cars to be more efficiently handled on the quayside and more quickly cleared through the customs. After experiments with the car ferry *Halladale* the Association was granted a licence to operate the equipment on a permanent basis.

However, the world encirclement of radio hardly needs a spotlight: and neither does the influence of the British Royal Family. None the less, when our roving beam moves on to 1950 it pauses over the occasion when HRH Princess Anne became the one millionth member, because she was born on the very day that figure was reached. Thus the ambition of many years was celebrated on a day when more than one pioneer cast his mind back to times when the million were only a hundred and the arm of the law lay heavily on them.

But 1950 was a fitting mid-century year in other ways. It saw, for instance, the recruitment of women to the AA's road staff – an opportunity provided by the London pilot scheme. Above all it ushered in a period of such general activity and prestige that only four years were to elapse before the Association recruited its one and a half millionth member – and so set a seal on its long labours which shall last until the two millionth member appears in due course. That this remarkable increase should have taken place under the Presidency of HRH the Duke of Edinburgh is a matter for pride throughout the entire organisation: for ever since 1951, when the Duke graciously consented to become President in succession to the late Duke of Devonshire (who had himself succeeded the Earl of Lonsdale), he had taken an active interest in the Association's affairs. And these could hardly have prospered more.

It is true, after all, that the amount of service given to its members and its public goodwill are as good a test of a social institution as the size of its membership list. So, if we look at the passage of these recent years, a great deal of worthy endeavour is revealed. In 1952, for instance, more than 97,000 members were assisted by the free breakdown service, over 20,000 by AA night breakdown vehicles in London, the midlands and Yorkshire, and over 30,000 by the free legal defence scheme. Moreover, almost 50,000 sets of documents were supplied to members taking their cars or motor cycles abroad;

almost 107,000 applications for shipment were handled; and arrangements were made for 5,000 vehicles to be flown across the Channel.

Such growth in any organisation would be extraordinary; and it
continued under new direction. Early in 1953 the death of Canon
Hassard-Short brought to the chairmanship Captain the Rt Hon Lord
Teynham, DSO, DSC, a distinguished retired naval officer who had
commanded destroyer and minesweeping forces during the invasion
of Europe by the allied armies. Some time previously Lord Teynham
had been elected to the committee of the Association, and was thus
familiar with its activities when he took office.

For a short time Lord Teynham and his fellow committee members
continued to enjoy the advice of William Gibson as Secretary – and
this was during a year of considerable activity. The radio patrols were
widely extended. North and west of the Caledonian Canal a new highland patrol came into operation with four-wheel-drive vehicles instead
of road service outfits. And on Coronation day the resources of the
Association were mobilised to smooth out traffic difficulties. Mobile
offices were stationed on the outskirts of London to guide visitors;
breakdown vehicles were sent out to help members and keep routes
free from obstruction; signposts were erected; maps were issued to
show the traffic regulations clearly. And William Gibson, whose
retirement was unhappily short lived, could leave the Secretary's
chair at the end of the year with a sense of satisfaction in the achievements of the body he had served so long.

Here it is impossible – in his own hearing, so to speak – to discuss
Gibson's successor, the fourth in the lineage of Secretaries, K. L.
Kelly. In appointing him the committee made a gesture of trust in
youth, since he had not even been born in the year of the Association's
foundation. It may, however, be said of him that his whole working
life has been spent in the service of the A A. Before the war he was
personal assistant to Edward Fryer and had worked in an area office.
During the war he served in the army. After demobilisation he became an assistant secretary to the Standing Joint Committee and head

of the Association's highways department. Now he counts it a great
honour to have the day to day steering of the A A in his hands as it
passes its fiftieth milestone.

To glance back for the last time, the Automobile Association in
1949 prepared a detailed signposting scheme for the London area,
where almost a quarter of Britain's inhabitants live. Agreed with the
Royal Automobile Club, and submitted to the Ministry of Transport
for approval, the scheme was handed to a working party on which the
A A was represented; and two years later a temporary plan was
brought into operation by which the A A posted its familiar yellow
signs everywhere in London north of the Thames. The working
party meantime continued its formidable task of devising a comprehensive system for London as a whole: and for this the Association's
signposting experts can claim credit, since the 'Through Route' signposting scheme which came into operation in the A A's jubilee year is
basically similar to its own original plans.

But here – with fresh signposts on the road and at the A A's own
golden milestone – we come to the end of this chapter of a story which
may itself still be only in its beginning. It started in days when motorists were denounced as 'demons in human shape' and cavalry
moustaches swayed like bushes in a strong wind at the slightest
sound of a motor car. Since then the internal combustion engine has
altered the social life of the nation by a transformation in which the
Automobile Association has played no unworthy part. For if some are
born great and others have greatness thrust upon them, there are also
those whose very struggle in a good cause makes them achieve greatness.

PLATE 13   *The first village sign erected by the Association (above): the celebrated Guards-to-Hastings run, re-enacted in jubilee year (left):*

the foundation of the aviation section (right): these are only three of the greater moments in the history of the A A.

II. ROUND THE CLOCK

RAYMOND BAXTER

This is the story of how the Automobile Association works today, told in the form of a log. The incidents factually reported below took place during a typical twenty-four hours recently – a normal, undramatic, mid-week, mid-season period – but they are of course only a selection, and half of them might have taken place in a single minute. They begin as the hands of the blue and gold clock in the reception room of Fanum House, London, part from the vertical as another day starts . . .

★   ★   ★   ★

00.03 The echoes of Big Ben have died away and an inspector of the London night breakdown service turns his Land Rover away from the Embankment to cross Westminster Bridge. As he drives quietly along he notices the rear lights of the car ahead flickering. Better follow it for a bit, he thinks, to see if it's just a loose connection or something more serious. For this is no time to run into electrical trouble, and it looks a bit foggy down towards London Bridge.

Ten minutes later the controller rises from the desk where he has been helping the watchkeeper to take cuttings from a late edition in which A A traffic figures are quoted. He crosses the room as the radio comes to life.

' . . . Hello, Fanum One. I am rectifying a rear light failure at the south end of Westminster Bridge. Member's name is Salmons. His number is D 107655. Yellow Item, Out.'

G

PLATE 14 *The car is ancient: the weather forecast is uncertain: and the bedroom windows have been forgotten. But the badge on the bonnet, at least, can be relied upon.*

'That's the lot for this one then.' The customs officer at
00.35   Western Docks, Dover, and the AA port officer on duty
there, complete their check on the documents. The AA
man crosses the customs hall, now almost deserted, walks the few
yards of quay to the gangway, and hands over a sheaf of papers to the
purser. Those papers deal with vehicles ranging from a motor scooter
owned by two students to a thirty-six seater coach bound for Vienna.

The white cuff of a dress shirt protrudes from a dinner
01.17   jacket as a hand reaches forward to press a starter but-
ton. There is a slight click, but no responding whirr of
motor. In the resonant tones of the East Riding a voice consigns all
such electrical devices to the devil, and an angry man steps from a car
outside a hotel in Newcastle.

A few moments later, as Patrol Jackson is comparing his fifteen
years on the roads of Northumberland astride a yellow motor cycle
with the comparative luxury of a Land Rover's cab, a loudspeaker
breaks his reverie. ' . . . Failure of starter. Position outside Great
Eastern Hotel. . . .'

'Good idea, carrying a special battery like that,' the man in the
dinner jacket is saying shortly afterwards. And, 'Aye,' answers
Patrol Jackson, 'that's the fourth time I've used it tonight. I think
you'll find that everything's all right now, sir.'

It is quite obvious that the load is too high to go under
02.34   the bridge. The driver and his mate gaze malevolently
at the offending parapet. A private car swishes past un-
heeding towards Bristol.

'Now what?' asks the mate. The driver spots the light of a telephone box in the dark village 200 yards ahead. 'I reckon I'll try the
AA,' he says.

'What'll they do? Move the bridge, or knock the top off the ruddy
transformer?'

'They might give us another route. What our guv'nor should have done. . . . '

And so in due course the lorry grinds slowly in reverse to a side road. With the expertise of the heavy-duty driver, the man at the wheel swings his load into the intersection, turns and is away.

'We go by Bath,' he says to his mate. 'The A A bloke said it's only about fifteen miles more anyway.'

03.16 The red glow of a rear light catches the eye straining along the yellow glare of the fog lamp. Visibility on Wimbledon Common is down to ten yards. The A A breakdown vehicle returning from another job stops smartly from its groping seven miles an hour. The driver jumps out and walks cautiously towards the rear light and dim outline of a saloon. 'Having trouble, sir?'

'Trouble? Am I glad to see you! How the blazes does one get to Kingston Vale from here? Or doesn't one try any more?'

'You should have turned left at the last roundabout, sir. By the way, this muck hasn't got there yet.' And the radio reports back: '. . . Hello, Fanum One. Proceeding to Kingston Vale, . . . guiding member's car. Position Tibbett's Corner, visibility ten yards. Yellow Able, out.'

Some minutes later: ' . . . Position Robin Hood Gate, Kingston by-pass. Visibility still ten yards. Yellow Able, over.' The radio controller glances at his map, checking the figure '10' over the area. 'Hello, Yellow Able. Thank you. Our chart shows forty yards on Kingston Hill. Please confirm this on your arrival. Fanum One, over.'

'Hello, Fanum One. Message understood. Roger. Yellow Able, out.'

The patrolman leans from the cab to call back to the following car. 'Cheer up, sir. We'll be out of this in ten minutes.' But all things are checked. 'Kingston police station? This is the A A. Would you mind telling me what visibility you have down by the river? . . . Thank you.' And this time a sinister '5' goes up on the visibility map as a creeping paralysis of fog closes in on a sleeping London.

04.51   There is no need for more than one warning clang of the bell as the fire engine shoots out into the deserted streets of Manchester. But a yellow sign and the word 'Diversion' catch the driver's eye, and the vehicle sweeps into a side road.

'What's this?'

'Dunno. A A sign said "Diversion". Got the road up in a big way, I suppose, though I must say I hadn't spotted it. Here's the next arrow. Right again. That's it. Straight back into Piccadilly. And . . . blimey, this looks quite a fire!'

05.30   A driver off the Night Ferry looks at his watch. 'How many miles to Arras on the A A route, darling?'

'The last village was Noeux-les-Something. It's fourteen miles to Arras. Shall we be in Paris for breakfast?'

'Sure. But it's just as well I had that route. Mind you, I still think it was worth getting cracking as soon as we docked.'

06.58   A garage door squeaks slightly as it swings open. A patrolman, dressed for the road, takes the oil can from the orderly array of tools on the bench and ministers to the hinge, for he is not a man to tolerate a squeaky door. As he checks fuel, tyres, oil and freedom of controls on his motor cycle combination he is content with the daily routine. Taking care of mechanical contrivances has always been his joy.

07.10   'The Automobile Association reports thick fog in South London and parts of Surrey,' reads the measured voice, 'which is slowing down traffic. Visibility in some districts is still restricted to fifteen yards. That is the end of the news. Now, here is a police message. . . .'

08.35   Above Leicester Square the canteen manageress checks her stocks and sees that more sugar is needed. She is responsible for 350 meals a day. The liftman is giving a final shine to his boots. The day of office work is almost ready to begin.

08.51   The London garage manager enters his domain from a world of dispersing fog and immediately takes a glance about him. One complete engine change, a brake and clutch overhaul, he thinks; that 'decoke' should be cleared today, but the valves need a regrind. He decides that he should be able to take two more vehicles in from the waiting list provided there are no major snags on the night service vehicles.

09.02   The first visitor of the day is greeted at the reception office in Maidstone – an Australian who wishes to tour the Old Country. Simultaneously, a switchboard girl puts through the first incoming call.

09.11   A builder at Cockfosters discovers a deserted car parked in his yard, and phones the police from his office. Then he takes another look at the car, notices an A A badge, reads the number on it, and telephones Whitehall 1200. Ten minutes later a further call is being put through.

'Thornton Heath 2166.'

'Good morning, sir. The Automobile Association here. Am I right in thinking that your car has been stolen?'

'Stolen? Hold on. I left it parked just round the corner to save the lights. I can see from the window if it's there. Hold on. . . . Lord, yes. My car's gone.'

'Well, don't worry, sir. It's in a builder's yard at Cockfosters, apparently undamaged. . . .'

09.34   In Glasgow office the area secretary and his area road manager are in conference. There is an application from the organising committee of a charity pageant for temporary road signs, two letters from members about a dangerous crossroads and badly sited signs, and a request from head office for a report on proposed Traffic Orders. Meanwhile a secretary is preparing the papers for a Ministry of Transport inquiry into a speed limit, a member is phoning for advice on the layout of a private parking place, and a genius is on his way up to explain his idea for reversing the direction of a car's fan in order to blow hot air forward and disperse fog.

09.55   At the patrols' training school near Nottingham an inspector watches the arrival of ten recruits. There are still nineteen due to report for the new course. Meanwhile his superior and a representative from head office are discussing the merits of new instructional films.

10.35   The chief clerk of Birmingham's free breakdown service is working his way through a pile of members' claims. The same area's technical department is dealing with a complex letter seeking advice on the economic operation of a fleet of vehicles, an irate caller announces that he has been robbed by an hotelier, and a member is being advised on the drafting of a letter to someone who has sold him a secondhand car with a doubtful back axle and temperamental ignition.

11.14   A Cadillac saloon draws up at Hounslow roundabout. The driver is bound for Southampton and the *Queen Mary*, but has to 'stop by' at Claridges to collect a business associate. He hates driving through London. 'The city's just a maze to me,' he says to the pretty girl awaiting him. Soon the Cadillac is under way again, the owner relaxed and confident. At his side an A A London pilot drives him along Hendon Way. 'Pleasant young woman, that,' thinks the American.

12.17 At head office a party of representatives from European motoring organisations, gathered together to inspect the A A's radio system, is being shown up by the reception room manager. A clerk in the road department is tracing a member's hat left at a café on the Minehead-Taunton road 'opposite a filling station', and on London's outskirts an area road manager is ringing the local authority's surveyor to point out the danger of mud spread on the road by lorries leaving a construction site. Signs department are working out plans for signposting a race meeting. A wheel, tyre, tube and front springs are being delivered to London Airport for despatch to a member in Germany who has crashed on the Hanover autobahn. A press officer is answering an enquiry from a motoring correspondent about the Association's views on a new 'no waiting' scheme. The drawing office is working on the plans of a dangerous road junction. The duplicating department is rolling out copies of an internal news sheet. The messengers are clearing the last hour's accumulation from the 'out' trays, and the uniform stores are despatching seventeen new greatcoats to patrols.

12.58 In the cold mountains of Wales a patrolman closes the gate of a field into which he has driven some wandering cows. He feels good because that morning he has signed up two new members – and because it is nearly time to get something warm inside him. But on his way to lunch he finds a subsidence in a secondary road harbouring several inches of water, and posts it with a red flag on either side.

14.43 'I was at first inclined,' concludes the magistrate, 'to take a serious view of this matter. But the very able pleading of the accused's solicitor has raised a real doubt in my mind. Case dismissed,' he says.

15.35   A telephone rings in the flat of a young married man. 'AA vehicle inspection here,' announces a decidedly Scots voice. 'I've just had a look at that pre-war model you were thinking of buying. You'll be getting our written report tomorrow, but as you said you were anxious to clinch the deal I'm ringing to let you know that the report won't be at all favourable.' The young man thanks the Scots voice and decides that, when you are about to spend most of the hard earned £200 in your bank on a car, a few of those pounds devoted to getting expert opinion is a very good investment.

16.40   'Hello, Fanum Six. Can you locate a replacement fan belt for a Czech car? A 1952 Skoda – spelt S-K-O-D-A.'
'. . . Let's see what technical department have to say.'
In a room lined with cupboards full of detailed data a drawer is opened and a file extracted. Then – 'Hello, Flame Dog. The nearest Rex garage may stock a fan belt which fits. Fanum Six, over.'
'Hello, Fanum Six. Roger. Flame Dog, out.'
And a little later the radio equipped patrolman speaks slowly to a man in a wide brimmed hat. 'We think we have found you a fan belt, sir. I shall now leave you in order to get it. I shall be back in fifteen minutes.'
'You are so very kind!'

17.30   Offices are closing. But many AA executives will be at their desks until much later, and files will be travelling home in brief cases all over the country as the Association's vigil continues.

20.20   The telephone enquiries are still flowing steadily in to night staffs. 'What is the nearest parking place for Olympia?' 'When was the man with the red flag abolished?' And 'Are there any motor cars in Tibet?'

PLATE 15

From weekend road scouts sponsored by private enthusiasts,

*through the first half-dozen regular patrols, and down to the days of
the powered
road service outfit –
such was the genesis
of the
A A patrol force,
whose story is told
a little later
in this book.*

22.00 The A A parliamentary officer leaves the chamber of the House of Lords. An amendment to a Road Traffic Bill has been under discussion: but whether it is a satisfactory one from the point of view of Britain's five million vehicle owners is hard to read from his face. He enters the lobby for a considered talk with fellow experts.

23.58 As the hands of the reception room clock close again, an inspector of the London night breakdown service crosses Westminster Bridge and swings his Land Rover eastwards along the Embankment. His assistance is required to discover why the engine of an invalid carriage refuses to start. He notices a trace of fog downstream towards London Bridge. . . .

　　　　★　　　★　　　★　　　★

And that is an outline of how the Automobile Association acts today as a major national institution. But it is only an outline. The rest of this book is here to fill in the details and to retail the dozen, the score, the hundred or the thousand A A stories which are all part of the story of the A A.

H

LATE 16 *Some members call in person at the reception hall of Fanum House: hers telephone its operations room. Between them they challenge the A A ith thousands of questions daily.*

III. ON PATROL

HOWARD MARSHALL

To the one and a half million British motorists who nowadays return his salute, the AA patrol is not so much a road scout as a combination of mechanic, guide, ambulance man, guardian angel and friend. So familiar a figure has he become that the nation pays him its highest compliment: it takes him for granted.

Yet throughout the British Isles (including even the Isle of Man and the Channel Islands) this figure – this weather tanned motor cyclist in the trim khaki uniform – represents one of the most remarkable social developments of our time. Despite his crisp, self confident bearing he has not one iota of legal authority; yet he can be found any day sorting out traffic tangles and road mishaps and his assistance is called for some two million times annually. Efficient but never officious, he is an acknowledged – but wholly unofficial – representative of law and order. His universally accepted right to this assumption of public duty is a measure of the status which, after half a century of service, the patrol now enjoys. It stands, too, for a very real contribution to our way of life.

Today, when the prestige of the AA is still increasing and its influence acknowledged all over the world, it is not easy to comprehend those struggles out of which the patrol service as we now know it was born. And it is not the least of our twentieth century paradoxes that from such piratical beginnings there should have stemmed an organisation not only accepted but welcomed by police and public alike.

The extent of the skirmishings of those early days is now a matter of history. Years afterwards the late Superintendent Drew (who is generally credited with being the Association's first patrol) recalled that the local police inspector on his beat even resorted to disguise in an effort to throw him off the scent. Despite the policeman's dark glasses, muffler and other melodramatic effects, Drew was always there when the inspector emerged, stopwatch at the ready, to lie in wait for unsuspecting speed merchants. 'The secret was,' he recalled, 'that everybody in the district was amused by my lone stand against the all-powerful inspector. And my intelligence service was such that he could not go out of his front door – or the back for that matter – without word reaching me in a few minutes. The people who lived next door to him, the butcher, the greengrocer and even the builder, were all on my side – and sometimes they would do the job for me if I was not on the spot.'

So, whether the police knew it or not, by 1909 (when membership had reached 10,000) the writing was on the wall. Motoring was there to stay – and with it the AA patrol.

Between 1910 and the outbreak of the Kaiser's war, relations between patrols and the authorities improved to such an extent that the concept of service from which the whole idea of the Association had originated could begin to be implemented in full. On roads throughout the country the distinctive combination of yellow and black, and the Association symbol, became widely familiar through patrols, road signs and other activities. And then too the first of the now familiar telephone boxes, of which members held the key, linked the stranded motorist with means of rescue, though their function caused perplexity to some. Long after the boxes had been installed, for instance, a member telephoned from one on the Oxford road complaining that he had opened it but could not find a patrol inside.

As for the men themselves, they began to assume, along with their new responsibilities, a new dignity. A uniform was designed for them – the smart serviceable tunic, the breeches and the polished boots which have distinguished them ever since. And when, after contributing their own special chapter to the history of the war, the patrols returned to the roads of Britain, the back of their enormous job was

already broken. Their story for the ensuing thirty years is the story
of the Association itself – of rising membership, of ever increasing
services, of enterprise rewarded and early faith justified.

'Surprisingly few people,' said the old *Daily News* in its issue of 6th
February 1913, 'realise how elaborately the road is organised in
these motoring days. It is no longer a free and easy highway where a
man may escape from the formalities of towns. Every day it becomes
more like a railway, a formal affair with officers constantly on duty, a
track arranged for speed.'

'The AA,' this paper continued, 'now employs 550 road patrols
and cheerfully spends £35,000 on their wages every year. In addition
there are the inspectors and superintendents and the outlay expenditure of the organisation is at least £40,000 a year . . . There is now
a patrol for every twelve miles of popular main road and in the country to the south of London there is a patrol about every six miles. The
whole organisation is surprisingly thorough. Not a car can go out of
London, except perhaps on an insignificant by-road, without the
knowledge of the AA. The patrols make a note of every car and even
every motor cycle that passes, whether a member's or non-member's;
and at the end of the week they send in records to headquarters giving
the number and colour of every car that passed a certain point, the
time it passed and the direction it was travelling . . . . Each patrol
holds a first aid certificate, keeps an outfit and is expected to be able
to do what is necessary in case of accident. Last year about 5,000
accidents were dealt with by the patrols and several lives saved.'

The report adds a note on the life of a patrol at that time: it was 'on
the whole enjoyable. The patrol,' added the newspaper, 'is in the open
air most of the day, and his work is not heavy . . . . He can earn about
26s a week and if he works up to the position of inspector or superintendent he can earn considerably more. With a cottage in a village he
does not do so badly. Numbers of men have taken up the work for the
sake of their health and several city workers have become different
men after six months on the road.'

That, remember, was written in February 1913, before the Association was eight years old. It has long since become impossible, even if it were necessary, to keep a check on every vehicle leaving London, though patrols may still estimate the volume of traffic on main roads at peak periods. But otherwise the shape of the patrols' duties and future development was already broadly determined. What lay ahead remained a challenge: but the biggest battle, the battle for acceptance, had been soundly won.

'The daily reports sent in by the road patrols,' commented *The Motor* in its issue of 25th March 1913, 'often refer to services of great value rendered to the general public and to the local authorities. Last week the roadside telephone sentry box at Maidenhead Thicket was freely used by the police in tracking down three burglars who were escaping across open country. For nearly two hours the patrol on duty was telephoning information to the police and the men were finally arrested in Cherry Garden Lane.'

Only a year later there appeared this note on yet another aspect of the patrols' daily round:

'In addition to their everyday work of assisting A A members who experience mechanical breakdowns with their cars, the road patrols are occasionally able to render assistance to aviators involuntarily alighting near their beats. Two aviators were recently assisted in one week. In one case a patrol saw an aeroplane descend into a wheat field. Its breakdown was due to a fractured petrol pipe. In landing damage was caused, and the patrol stood by while repairs were effected, gave assistance, and kept the road clear for passing traffic. In the second case, an Army aeroplane made a sudden descent into a field. When the patrol rode up he found that the trouble was a leaking petrol tank. He procured from the nearest repairing establishment, fresh supplies of petrol, oil, also replacements.'

The activities of patrols as special road police were illustrated in an article in *The Motor* dated 23rd November 1915. 'A patrol on duty in Hertfordshire,' said the report, 'found a drunken man on his beat who was extremely dangerous to passing traffic. He utilised his sentry box telephone and called for a police constable to take the man in charge. Another patrol was instrumental in recovering a stolen bicycle and tracing the thief. A patrol in the Gloucester district found over 100 yards of his beat covered with broken glass. He borrowed a broom from a nearby cottage and carefully swept the whole length.'

(AA members are asked always to enquire the reason if no salute is given by the uniformed patrol.)
Short sighted new owner (to general in full uniform waiting for the country bus). 'NOW THEN, MY MAN - NOW THEN! WHY NO SALUTE?'

None of these instances would be in any way unusual forty years later, though the frequency with which cases of straying cattle were reported at that time has inevitably dwindled. For, as the years passed, the patrols' place in the community became ever more prominent and the services of the Association ever more closely identified with the daily life of a rapidly expanding society. Far from being at odds with the law, patrols now co-operated with local policemen. When a motorist from overseas killed a child on the Southampton

road it was the alacrity of the patrols along the route which led to
his capture at the docks, on the very liner which might otherwise have
carried him beyond reach of the law. (He was subsequently sentenced
to two years' imprisonment.) The recovery of stolen cars through the
sharp eyes and quick wits of patrols became commonplace; and general traffic control, especially at busy holiday seasons, became a part
of the patrols' duties accepted by police and public alike.

But this is not to say that the Association encouraged its servants to
assume police responsibilities. At the time of the car bandit scares of
1932 the Association told the press that it was perfectly prepared to
help the police combat the menace 'to the fullest extent', while retain-
ing control of both its staff and its telephone boxes. 'Our patrols,' this
statement added, 'have already assisted the police on hundreds of
occasions, but the prevention of crime or the apprehension of criminals
does not come within the scope of our activities and there is no suggestion now that our patrols are to try to detain suspects.'

In March of the following year the Essex police sought to augment
their strength by enlisting patrols as special constables. The Association refused. 'We do a great deal of public service in addition to the
work of members,' said an official statement at the time, 'but it should
be remembered that the A A patrols are on duty to assist members by
whom they are paid . . . . If we were to allow our patrols to be controlled by the police, the position in which they might find themselves
would be impossible.'

The solution, like so many of the best ones, was a compromise:
commonsense and a well developed feeling for public duty have provided the answer ever since.

Writing in September 1931, Stenson Cooke declared that the
patrols were chosen 'for their courtesy, instant action in all emergencies, knowledge of road maps, road sense, endurance, coolness, ability
to do ordinary repairs and general capacity for saying and doing the
right thing at the right moment.' To this formidable list of qualifications he added: 'We pick a dozen out of any 100 who apply – and

even then they go through a month's probation.' Further, Mr Cooke revealed that 'on a bicycle the road scout patrols eight miles; on a motor cycle combination his beat is twenty miles . . . . He costs us hundreds of thousands of pounds a year in telephone calls.' Woman, declared the Secretary, 'took up motoring largely because of the knowledge that the road scout would be by her side in any case of trouble. She now smokes a cigarette until he arrives.' He dismissed the idea that the AA might introduce women road scouts. 'We thought of it once,' he admitted, 'but decided against. It's men's work.'

Few would quarrel with those sentiments, and it is interesting to see how little the definition of a patrol's abilities has varied over the years. But there have been many technical advances, of course, of which the most impressive is perhaps the use of radio.

The Association had for many years contemplated the eventual use of radio as a means of improving their services still further, but it was not till 1951 that the success of its radio controlled night breakdown service, described elsewhere, prompted it to embark on a nationwide scheme to equip its normal road patrols with two-way sets. The intention was that a member whose vehicle broke down would merely telephone his local AA office for help, whereupon the patrol nearest the scene of the breakdown could be directed straight to him by radio. Other advantages of the system would include up to the minute weather reports and machinery for dealing with traffic congestion.

There were undeniable difficulties. The site for each transmitter had to be not only in a suitably commanding position, but also within a fifteen mile radius of the control room (for connection with it by land line) and within convenient reach of power supplies. Nevertheless, once the technical snags had been overcome the new scheme was a complete success. In conjunction with the radio controlled night breakdown service it began by providing a round-the-clock coverage of the London district, extending some twenty to twenty-five miles out into the surrounding suburbs. Guildford was the first of the provincial areas to be equipped, and the service has subsequently been

" Before I start, are you one of these chaps who kick up hell at our Annual General Meetings? "

Collar black.
Sleeve titles gold on black.
1 wide and 2 narrow black rings on
plain cuff. (Also worn by
Superintendent Port Officers.)

Sleeve titles gold on red.

Sleeve titles gold on black.
Collar black. Cuffs as for Chief Inspector.
Port Officer in Charge,
as above but 1 wide black ring on plain cuff.

Collar black.
Sleeve titles yellow on black.
1 wide black ring on plain cuff.
Assistant Port Officer,
as above but plain cuff with no rings.

Collar black.
Sleeve titles gold on black.
1 wide and 1 narrow black ring on
plain cuff. (Also worn by
Chief Port Officers.)

(Ireland only)

S O M E   T Y P I C A L   I N S I G N I A   O F

Cap badge for Superintendents and Chief Inspectors.

Inspectors,
Gold badge
on red collar.
Cuffs plain.

Cap badge for Inspectors, Sergeants and Patrols.

Patrol's collar.
Yellow badge and piping on black.

Sergeant's chevrons.

Yellow on black.
Worn on right arm only.

Long service stars and chevrons.

1 star for every 20 years' service.

1 gold chevron for every 10 years' service.
1 silver chevron for every 5 years' service.

Worn on left arm only.

OFFICE, RANK AND SERVICE

extended to Glasgow, Birmingham, Leeds, Newcastle, Manchester, Nottingham, Bristol and Cambridge. Now, in the Association's jubilee year, over 100 radio patrols cover tens of thousands of square miles, including some of the most densely populated areas in the country. The day is not far distant when virtually every part of the United Kingdom will be covered by the A A's radio network.

For the patrol himself these developments are exciting enough. True, they make new demands on his initiative, but that is just the quality for which he is selected. Unlike the normal patrols, the radio equipped ones do not follow a regular 'beat' but range wherever a summons may call them. Not infrequently this means that they cross into territory which is not, strictly speaking, within their 'home' area; but that very elasticity is one of the particular strengths of the radio patrol system.

It takes more than a casual glance to distinguish a radio patrol from any other: the aerial is not particularly conspicuous and the uncomplicated radio set and batteries are compactly housed in the patrol's sidecar, with the handset alongside. Each patrol is equipped with two sets of batteries which are used one day at a time, the second of the pair being meanwhile charged from the mains. As the A A patrol garages and maintains his own combination, this adds yet another out-of-hours duty to his daily task. But even patrols who live in country areas where there is no mains electricity find a way.

Each patrol has his own call sign – a colour, common to all stations in his particular area, followed by an initial. When he hears his call sign ('Fanum Two calling Crimson George. I have a message for you. Over.') he stops his machine, picks up the handset from beside the radio, and transmits his reply. In order to enable him to pick up a message even when at some small distance from his motor cycle combination – for example, when attending to a breakdown – reception is through a loudspeaker.

These developments – and the complementary use of 'walkie-talkie' sets – seem typical of the way in which the AA not merely keeps in step with the times but often gets a little ahead of them. 'In this sort of organisation,' an inspector told me, 'you feel that there is something really powerful at the back of you – a driving force which is for ever turning out new ideas and putting them into practice. It's something to live up to, I can tell you.'

By the same token the patrol, like any other man with skill at his fingertips, is never bored. 'You can be cruising along on your beat,' one of them told me, 'with your thoughts miles away, when suddenly something attracts your attention. It may be obvious, like a car stuck at the side of the road with the bonnet up, or it may not be so obvious – a spot of oil on the road, or a rabbit dying of myxomatosis. And suddenly you are in action – looking for the fault, wiping up the oil, or putting the rabbit out of its misery. It's all in the day's work.'

All in the day's work. . . . That is a phrase one hears over and over again when speaking to patrols on the miles of road which they cover. The variety of the incidents they encounter is as wide and as varied as life itself. Chasing a couple of handcuffed prisoners; finding a bed for a chimpanzee or rounding up forty tortoises; delivering a baby in a snowstorm; saving a would-be suicide or discouraging a would-be murderer; administering first aid to a motor cyclist whose leg has been severed in an accident – these are only some of the experiences, quite often aiding non-members, which a few minutes' conversation with patrols on the beat brings to light. 'We get a lot of funny things happen to us,' one said, 'but after a while you come to accept them as nothing out of the ordinary.'

It depends, of course, upon your definition of the ordinary. For example, a young patrol of some twelve months' service was on relief duty one Sunday morning deep in the west country when the telephone in his box rang. Across the wire came a message to stop a car which was on its way from London to Bath. As the line was bad, the patrol concentrated all his attention on taking down the message correctly; and when he heard a heavy step on the gravel outside the box, followed by a nudge in the back, he could spare time to say only, 'One moment, sir', before returning his attention to the telephone. Just then he felt something rummaging in his pocket. He glanced over his shoulder to confront the pickpocket and found himself face to face with an elephant. He looked again and found a second one, a junior edition, close behind. 'I tried to think,' reported the patrol later, 'of any paragraph in the patrol guide which might cover this eventuality.' The situation was saved by the sudden appearance of a little brown skinned man with a turban. His opening words, however, were spoken not in Hindustani but in broad Cockney: 'How far is it to Chippenham, mate? These blasted animals have walked me off me plates.'

Zoological experiences – extending even to the succouring of swans – seem from the beginning to have figured prominently in the patrols' daily round. It was another elephant that prompted a harassed and anxious lorry driver, whose passenger the beast was, to appeal to a passing patrol for help: it was stamping its feet with alarming violence and threatening to smash through the floor boards. The patrol called out the local fire brigade with a suggestion that a sudden drenching from a hose might cool the elephant down. It failed to do so: and suddenly, with a resounding crash, the animal sank from view. It took a huge crane, a special sling and all the patrol's ingenuity to lift the elephant clear of the wreckage.

At the opposite end of the animal scale there is the story of the Bedford patrol who came to the rescue of five ladies whom he found at bay beside a stationary car. Each of them was crudely armed with sticks or pieces of board. One of them wielded a heavy book. The sight of the patrol dismounting to investigate gave them the courage to shout 'It's a mouse! In our car!' The patrol found the intruder, which the ladies told him belonged to a small boy at whose house they had stopped some hours previously. When the grateful ladies at last boarded their car and set off again the patrol departed in the opposite direction – to return the mouse to its owner.

Temerity of a different kind was once demanded of an inspector in the Doncaster district who, while on car parking duty at a Long Eaton circus, suddenly heard a call for help coming from the arena. The inspector was on his way to investigate when he came face to face with a lion. He leapt astride his combination one bound ahead of the animal and got off to a flying start. The roar of the engine scared the lion, which promptly set off in the opposite direction. The inspector chased it round and round the field until it collapsed in sheer exhaustion. The inspector's own state of health by that stage is not recorded.

Service with a smile is not, apparently, always easy to achieve: for there are a few members who have much in common with man-eating lions. One choleric motorist, for instance, refused to believe the patrol who told him that the cause of his breakdown was not ignition but petrol trouble. 'Whose car is this – yours or mine?' the driver demanded. 'Petrol be damned – it's ignition trouble!' And he accompanied these remarks with thunderous blows of his fist on the wing of the offending car. Eventually, after threatening to report the patrol for inefficiency, the driver allowed him to proceed with his examination of the fuel system. It was not until the patrol had plumbed the petrol tank to convince the driver that he had in fact run out of petrol that the situation was saved. Nevertheless, this driver was one of those who like to have the last word. Just as the engine burst into life he thrust his head out of the window and said 'I don't care what you say – coil ignition is no damned good!'

That gentleman would have found something in common with the west country member who, stuck on a steep hill on Dartmoor, refused to believe the patrol who assured him that the fault did not lie with either engine or transmission. When the patrol suggested that the driver had possibly failed to engage bottom gear, the reply was couched in terms too lurid to be repeated. However, the patrol at last persuaded the member to let him try, and to the accompaniment of a caustic and disparaging commentary he sat himself at the wheel. A manipulation of the gear lever, an easing of the handbrake, and the car moved smoothly off to the top of the hill. When the discomfited owner caught up with him, the patrol had the rare pleasure of demon-

THE FRIEND IN NEED.

"HELLO—A BREAKDOWN? ALLOW ME, MADAM. I KNOW ALL ABOUT THESE TITANS."

THE ROOT OF THE TROUBLE IS OFTEN DIRTY PLUGS OR CARBURETTOR CHOKED.

BUT IN THIS CASE IT MAY BE A STOPPAGE IN THE WATER CONNECTION.

OR, OF COURSE, IT MAY BE THAT YOUR BIG ENDS HAVE RUN OUT.

OR THERE IS JUST A CHANCE THAT YOUR GEAR-BOX SELECTOR IS JAMMED.

AND WHILE WE'RE AT IT WE MAY AS WELL MAKE SURE THAT THE UNIVERSAL JOINTS HAVEN'T GOT TORN OUT.

BUT IN ANY CASE IT CAN'T BE ANYTHING SERIOUS. I SHOULD JUST WAIT TILL AN A.A. MAN COMES ALONG."

strating how to engage first gear – for the member had never realised
that his was a four speed gearbox. The patrol's report ends – pleas-
antly enough – 'Apologies, a smile, a salute . . . and off went another
satisfied customer.'

Such peculiarities, indeed, can usually be dealt with gracefully. A
case in point occurred during the blackout years, when a patrol had
to pay a late duty visit on a raw and windy night. He knocked on the
side door and a woman's voice from inside shouted 'Who is it?' He
answered and explained his business. Gingerly the woman opened the
door, and the instant she set eyes on the patrol in his oilskin suit she
shouted over her shoulder to her husband 'George, come quickly! It's
a German paratrooper!' The husband emerged, crying 'Speak English or I'll shoot!' The patrol passed several anxious seconds before
he was able to convince the householders that he was on peaceable
business. And then, catching sight of himself in a mirror, the explanation struck him. His face was streaked with blood where the rambler
rose outside had lashed against him in the gale.

And then there is the story of the patrol who was able to help a
lady to mend a hole in her stocking. At the autumn meeting at Aintree
a very smartly dressed woman reversed her drophead coupé into
position, switched off the engine, and deliberately set out to catch the
eye of a nearby patrol who was supervising the car park. When he
approached her she asked 'Have you a needle and thread? There's a
hole in the heel of my stocking and I simply dare not walk into the
grandstand with it'. The patrol had neither needle nor thread. But he
was able to produce a piece of court plaster which both matched the
shade of the stocking and repaired it neatly. It is said that, ever since,
patrols have made a point of carrying needle and thread along with
the many other essential items packed into the sidecars of those
familiar motor cycle combinations which are known in the trade as
road service outfits or RSOs.

A more recent instance of running repairs is reported by a patrol
who found himself ministering not to a lady member but to a road

sweeper. This unfortunate citizen was stooping down to gather sweepings into his shovel when a car, drawing close alongside, ripped open the seat of his pants with a door handle. The driver leaned out and asked his victim the way to Ormesby, but received in return 'explicit instructions' (in the patrol's own words) 'to go somewhere else'. The patrol concluded: 'I was able to get to the seat of the trouble and stepped into the breach with pins from my first aid outfit. Now they call me the A A's "pin-up boy"'.

But patrols, of course, are usually resourceful men. There was the one who was standing in a country road not far from where a horse thrust his head over a fence when a Daimler drew up containing four ladies in riding habits. 'I don't suppose,' called the driver, 'that the A A provide their men with sugar so that members can feed horses?' With a straight face the patrol replied 'Certainly, madam' – and promptly produced two lumps from his pocket. As he rode off she was still gazing dumbfounded at the sugar in her hand. She was not to know – and the patrol very rightly did not tell her – that the sugar was an emergency measure against the parsimony of wayside cafés.

Paradoxically enough, it is when the weather is at its worst and only dire necessity keeps motorists on the road that the patrol comes into his own, for the weather plays a large part in his duties. One can imagine the feelings of the patrol who, speaking from his telephone box as part of the Association's road-weather service, had to report heavy floods in his district. On being told to speak up, as he was not coming through distinctly, he explained he was lying flat on the roof of a box which was five feet deep in water.

Often enough, as is told later, the patrols' reports on flooded rivers and overflowing lakes have helped to establish a nationwide network of relief: and often enough, too, they have been called on to operate that network. Rescue operations, diversion signs, traffic control – all these are part of the patrols' normal stock in trade. But individual initiative comes into it too, as the report of a patrol in north Wales underlines most vividly.

'At approximately 6.15 pm,' he wrote – and note the time, for it was after normal duty hours, 'I started off on my RSO for Bethesda, travelling very cautiously and passing through long stretches of flood water. On rounding a bend about one mile from the lake I ran into a foot of water and picked up in my headlights two cars and a van about forty yards ahead. It was impossible to go back, owing to the fact that huge boulders were falling down the mountainside behind me. So I drove forward a few more yards, when suddenly the water rose to the level of my saddle. Hearing a child's voice in the darkness ahead, I dismounted and waded forward with the water rising practically to shoulder level. I made my way to one car, which was occupied by an invalid A A member and his family, including a young boy who was very frightened. I told them they were in no danger, helped to push the car out of the flood water, and told the driver to wait until I returned with help. After checking the other vehicles and finding they had been abandoned, I then pushed my RSO out of the deep water and drove down to the village of Bethesda, where I immediately advised the police and arranged for the main road to be closed.'

Such stories add up to a picture of an amazingly varied job. Rescuing animals; buying and delivering a radio set for a 'CB' national serviceman; having a fight with a lunatic; recovering lost or stolen property; being struck by lightning; patching up stranded aircraft; minding a member's baby – the list is inexhaustible, and increases with every issue of the patrols' own news letter. The patrol, then, has to be a man of infinite resource; and in times of emergency his training and experience are beyond price.

The armed forces of two world wars, for instance, have found in the patrols recruits with trained minds and skilled hands, who are moreover already imbued with an instinctive sense of discipline. It is no surprise that so many of them, in the last war, found their way into the Royal Military Police. Indeed, the link between the A A and this branch of the services has become a tradition, based on outstanding service during the wars and maintained today by the two emergency

PLATE 17 *A man must undergo a rigorous and intensive course of trainin at the A A's own school before he acquires a beat of his ow and becomes that familiar and friendly figure, the patro*

*At Widmerpool Hall
near Nottingham,
recruits, and veteran patrols
on refresher courses,
inspect mechanisms,
attend lectures
and study
traffic difficulties.*

PLATE 18

The alert and disciplined precision of the patrols is emphasised by these two photographs, taken when the

PLATE 19

Out in all weathers,
the A A patrols help
to keep Britain's traffic
on the move.

took delivery of new road service outfits, which, like their headgear (above), have since been improved.

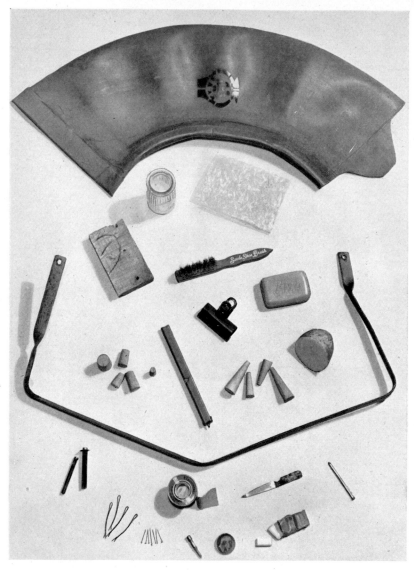

PLATE 20   *Old iron, corks, pins, potatoes, paper clips,*
paste jars and pennies . . . these are some of the objects patrols have
used in improvised emergency repairs.

reserve companies of the Royal Military Police which are composed almost entirely of volunteers from the patrol staff. To the men concerned this is both a voluntary form of spare time national service and a unique opportunity for them to get together and enjoy the kind of comradeship which, by the very nature of their job, is normally denied them. Other patrols during the second war quickly found themselves in command of tanks, aircraft or transport columns. Workshops and depots all over the world remember the man – usually a senior NCO or warrant officer – whose mechanical skill and experience came from civvy street, from those highways of faraway Blighty which he once patrolled in a khaki uniform of a different kind.

Nowhere, perhaps, is the AA man thrown so much on his own resources as in the wilds of Scotland. Even the motorists most in love with rugged highland scenery have reservations about rugged highland roads, and these certainly present a special problem to the patrol organisation. As opposed to the normal RSO system, the Association now (as a post-war development) operates a highland patrol of specially equipped Land Rovers, painted and fitted out after the familiar pattern. Their beats, lying between Durness and John o' Groats in the north and Invermoriston, Invergary and Kyleakin in the south, link up with the normal patrols covering the highways through Inverness up to Golspie and total nearly 1,000 miles.

These patrols have been somewhat picturesquely styled the storm-troops of the Scottish roads; and certainly, even during the tourist season in which they operate, they are exposed to variations of weather scarcely to be encountered anywhere else in the British Isles. Scotland's highland tracks are mostly narrow, and surface conditions vary considerably, particularly on the west coast. The AA believes it its business to open up the remoter fastnesses of Scotland to motorists who, in the past, have been deterred by the lack of maintenance and repair facilities. The Land Rovers, therefore, follow regular daily beats and are, of course, more comprehensively equipped with breakdown equipment than RSOs can be.

The men who operate the highland patrol are mostly natives of the country and as often as not of the particular districts in which they operate, but even so they might well be forgiven an occasional pang of loneliness. Each covers over 150 miles a day, and those miles are liable to be uneventful. Nevertheless, they do much to link the remoter parts of the country with what, even in those parts, is called 'civilisation'. In the highlands it is no uncommon thing for public telephones to be ten miles apart, and garages up to fifty. The patrol, in such circumstances, takes on a new responsibility. Some crofters even declare that they tell the time by him.

Highland weather is like no other weather in the British Isles, and the patrolmen there get used to describing torrential downpours as 'a little low cloud'. At least one A A man has saved a life in those bitter blizzards which can sweep down from the north in a Scottish winter. It was, says a Lanarkshire patrol, 'just instinct' that made him stop his Land Rover a year or two ago and look into a snow filled ditch. There, dimly discernible, was a motor cycle; and as the Scot turned back to his machine to fetch a tow line, his eye caught a faint movement. The rider was pinned underneath, helpless and injured. It was only the patrol's trained eye, and his highly developed sixth sense, which saved that rider's life.

A less dramatic and rather odder affair came the way of the patrol who heard that a body had been spotted not far from a nearby railway line and appeared to have fallen from a train. The patrol went to the scene and found the ragged, rain soaked body of a middle aged woman lying there, rigid and frozen. He applied artificial respiration, and at long last signs of life appeared. The patrol continued until the woman was able first to stand and then to move, whereupon she revealed that she and her husband were 'on tramp' and that he had left her the night before. From her description the patrol recognised her husband who had (he told her) spent the night in a hay shed some four miles further on. The last he saw of her she was in pursuit of her errant spouse, muttering oaths of vengeance.

The size of Scotland does not always impress itself upon visiting motorists. An American lady who recently stopped a patrol there opened a conversation with 'Say, we've come up to see the Scottish highlands. Where do we go?' The patrol asked her how long a tour she had in mind. 'Well,' said the American, 'I have to be back in Edinburgh by 5.30 this evening to meet my husband.' The sequel was that, on the patrol's advice, she spent a thoroughly enjoyable afternoon watching some highland games.

Across the Irish Sea, also, the helping hand extends. In the opening chapter of this book reference has been made to the early history of the Association in Ireland; but the motoring conditions obtaining in 1910 are worth recalling here, for they were probably the worst of any in the British Isles. The rough, flinty roads spelt ruin to pneumatic tyres; broken springs were universally regarded as inevitable penalties for motoring on Irish roads: and in the whole length and breadth of the island there was scarcely a single signpost.

One by one these problems were tackled and overcome, and soon after the first war a small band of patrols took to the road. Gradually there has evolved a national patrol system similar to that operating throughout Great Britain. The country is divided into two A A areas, with headquarters at Belfast and Dublin, separated by the political frontier; but the service given under both flags is the familiar one.

In fact, whether they believe in leprechauns or not, Irish motorists
have long since become accustomed to the AA patrol's particular
kind of magic – which in those lonely parts may include breaking open
a jammed safe, buying a goat, or advancing money to an impecunious
schoolboy. But, as an additional service to members, the Association
is now experimenting with Land Rovers after the patrolling pattern
which has worked so well in the Scottish highlands. These are in wide
demand in those parts of the country where garages and breakdown
services are still very far apart, and where even the wayside telephone
is something of a rarity.

But everywhere in the four kingdoms and the one republic instances
of the patrol's skill and resource are beyond computing. The number
of injuries tended by patrols in the course of their daily duties and the
number of lives saved, for instance, mounts steadily. Like so much of
the patrol's contribution to our motoring welfare, this particular aspect of public service is based on voluntary effort: it is in his evenings,
in his hard earned spare time, that the patrol attends classes at the
local Red Cross or St John Ambulance centre. His competence at first
aid makes him a particularly valued member of his community: he is
almost as likely to be called from his bed as the local nurse or midwife
– and not infrequently for the same purposes. Yet it is the lighter side
of the patrols' first aid experiences which particularly appeals to one
when listening to their stories.

During an icy spell a couple of years ago, for instance, a patrol was following a slowly moving motor cycle when it suddenly skidded. A second later the rider lay trapped by his left leg under the fallen machine. The patrol at once rushed up and, as he pulled the rider from under his motor cycle, saw that his left leg was grotesquely twisted. Even while his first aid drill flashed through his mind, however, the casualty took matters into its own hands by grabbing a terribly distorted knee and giving it a savage twist. The leg at once resumed a less alarming position. 'Seems all right,' muttered its owner, rolling up his trouser leg to reveal an artificial limb with only a slight dent in it. A moment later he was on his way. It was the patrol himself who felt in need of a stiffener. . . .

And what *of* the patrol himself – the man on the road? What kind of a person can he be? What are his qualifications? What does he get out of this open air life of his, in which every waking moment is at the immediate disposal of others? In an attempt to answer these questions I went out on to some of the busiest roads in the home counties, meeting and talking to whichever patrols came my way. To think of them collectively is, strictly speaking, impossible: any company of men, whatever their calling, must vary in type and personality. Nevertheless, I have formed a definite impression of the 'typical' AA patrol, just as, I imagine, the majority of motorists have formed impressions of their own.

First, every one of the patrols I met had upon him the stamp of *character*: here was no ill-defined personality, but a man sure of himself and of his ability to carry out his duties. Second, I was impressed by the awareness of *discipline* – a discipline submitted to willingly as a basic essential of a tricky and responsible job. Third, the patrol is a *conscientious* man who never closes his eyes to an incident which can only mean work for him. And, fourth, I was struck by a quality I recall having met previously in crack fighting units during the last war: a quality I can most nearly define as *confidence*.

These, I know, are generalities; but in the case of the A A patrol there are, I feel sure, at least one and a half million people of like mind to my own. Put to the test, these qualities manifest themselves in a bewildering variety of ways. The patrol's eyes, agents of a keen and highly trained brain, miss nothing. Despite his well chosen kit of tools his greatest assets are his fingers; and these fingers, thoroughly schooled in the intricacies of mechanical engineering, are nimble and ingenious. The patrol knows how to perform such difficult feats as starting a car which has been deliberately immobilised, or, without forcing a lock, getting into a vehicle whose owner has lost the key. He knows how to mend a broken feed pipe with a bit of transparent wrapping. He can turn a torch battery into an electric soldering iron, or a fish paste jar into a pump filter.

The basic qualifications, therefore, apart from distinct qualities of character, are mechanical aptitude and physical fitness. Upon the first of these can be imposed a thorough training: upon the second depends the candidate's ability to withstand the perversities of our climate and the feats of strength which he may be called upon to perform.

Selection of potential patrols is searching and thorough. If a man's background is satisfactory he is given a practical mechanical test by an area inspector. If he passes, he is then interviewed and tested by the local superintendent; and he is eventually taken on only after a stiff medical examination and a down to earth interview with the area secretary. 'It does not always occur to a candidate,' one area secretary told me, 'that a patrol's job keeps him away from home. It may even involve moving to a new district; and it certainly will if the man should be promoted, for we very rarely appoint an inspector to an area where he has already served as a patrol. Before any new candidate signs on, therefore, I ask him how his wife feels about his joining the AA. Will it matter to her that her husband henceforth will work straight through the weekends, except when the rota gives him his three days off in each fourteen? Will she mind that he is liable to be called out at night despite the fact that his working day officially ends at dusk? In an organisation like ours, you see, service to our members can never be made to conform to the sort of hours and conditions of work laid down in some professions.'

The new patrol, then, can from the beginning harbour no delusions. His is no soft job, and it is made clear to him that it amounts in effect to a particular attitude to life. It is a curiously individual existence: it is not, unlike many another of the more rewarding vocations, a team job. But it does bring with it its own rewards, its own gratifications. 'It gets into your blood,' said a fifty year old veteran who has been patrolling the same beat for twenty years. 'And you can't get it out.'

This is a point of view shared by other patrols whom I met and spoke to. Many of them have come back into the Association after reaching high rank in the services during the war. One had left the

Association for a job in a garage, realised his mistake, and gone back. Another joined as a lad of twenty and expects to retire, he says, only when 'I'm too feeble to hitch my leg across the saddle'. All assured me that theirs was 'a job well worth doing'.

Possibly you have wondered who does the gardening round the AA phone boxes, who tends those gay flower beds and whitewashes the stone border. By now you will guess that it is none other than the patrol himself. The box on his beat – to which he must report at intervals for telephone contact – is his responsibility, and with it the little garden in which it stands. In this connection, a Yorkshire patrol recently caught two young boys picking daffodils from the flower beds around his box. 'Instead of ticking them off,' he reported later, 'I spoke to them as man to man, explaining how I took special care of my little garden, and why. The boys apologised and promised not to take my flowers any more.' This enlightened technique paid an unexpected dividend: next morning, when the patrol arrived at his box, he found it ablaze with daffodils, stuck in the soil, the fence, and the cracks of the door. 'Of course,' concluded his report thoughtfully, 'the boys only promised not to take *my* daffodils any more. . . .'

Though the patrolman's official day is from nine to seven in summer and from nine to lighting-up time in winter, averaging forty-four hours a week, he may have to work long hours at holiday times and his wife has come to expect him, as the saying goes, when she sees him. So much, indeed, is he at the public's call that even when taking a regulation tea break he must leave his RSO in such a position as to draw attention to his whereabouts. But in his home town or village the AA man is a popular and respected figure, enjoying a status given to few of his neighbours. Indeed, so well established do many become in their own locality that it is often not easy to move them to another: the local community complains to the Association, supported by motorists who strongly object to their old friend's posting.

And how do the patrolmen themselves view their work? 'I took on this job,' one of them told me, 'because when I was demobilised I was

PLATE 21 *The highlands of Scotland are beautiful, and sometimes cru*
But even to these lonely roads the AA service extends through its highland patro

PLATE 22

From the period of lightweight
road service outfits and the fashions
of the twenties (above left) has evolved
today's mechanised patrol force
with its use of radio for the
control of parking (above right)
and the direction of help (right).

The knight errant on patrol
is never off duty.
Even on his way home he may
have to improvise a wheel change
for a damsel in distress.

The *A A* service
is not restricted to members,
nor even to human beings.
*A lame dog, a horse whose life
could only be saved by rigging up a sling,
even a troop of circus elephants
crossing a road* – all these have found the patrol a friend in need.

PLATE 23

looking for a useful and worthwhile career. I'd done my share of office
work before joining up and the indoor life never suited me. Now I
reckon I'm twice the man I was – and twice as happy.' That man's
sentiments are not his alone, for the patrol force contains veterans
whose reluctance to retire sometimes embarrasses their super-
iors in the service.

But for a man to have the right make-up to become a patrol is not
enough, and to find out what else he must have I spent an interesting
day at the A A's own training school at Widmerpool Hall, through
which every new patrolman must pass. In the lecture room there a
prominent notice is displayed. It reads: 'You have inherited a proud
tradition. You must uphold it'. Tradition is something which money
cannot buy and which even time cannot of itself establish. But at Widmerpool Hall it strikes visitor and pupil alike – that unique mixture
of discipline and courtesy which the A A has made its own. Here at the
training school the Association's principles are the mainspring of the
syllabus. 'The patrol service,' wrote a former Secretary of the Association, 'is the backbone of the A A – always has been and always will
be. We are determined therefore to create a uniformly high standard
of service – and that cannot be achieved unless the patrols, the men
actually on the job on the roads, are one hundred per cent trained for
their work. This school . . . is the answer.'

Each course lasts ten days and is attended by about thirty men. The
curriculum includes the location and correction of mechanical and electrical faults, maintenance drills, road safety, traffic control and practical demonstrations of all kinds. Brisk efficiency is the order of the
day, developing quick wits and lively minds among the students.
Classes take part in mock accidents, in which both their technical skill
and their first aid drill are put to the test. They dismantle and reas-
semble their road service outfits, they perfect their driving technique
and road drill, they learn to handle crowds and 'difficult' traffic. And
so detailed is their preparation for the job they will be doing that
Widmerpool Hall even boasts a demonstration explosive escape seat

PLATE 24 *The inns of Britain are rich in history and association.*
The golden sign which hangs above so many of them also has an honourable past.

from a jet aeroplane, in order that, should a patrolman find a pilot trapped in one, he will know how to rescue him without blowing both parties to blazes.

During this intensive period recruits are also shown how to keep their RSOs clean and tidy and their personal equipment spotless. They are taught map reading on enormously blown-up ordnance survey maps. They get out on the roads round Nottingham to gain experience, and they make daily reports for inspection by their instructors. They are taught the right ways of contact with members – for there is a right way and a wrong way to approach a driver who asks for help. The patrol needs, indeed, to be something of a psychologist: and he learns that courtesy, keenness and promptitude never fail to establish cordial relationships. There is no clemency at the school for slackness or inattention: and in the film that is regularly shown to recruits there are amusing incidents of how *not* to behave when on patrol. Never, they learn, park your RSO outside a public house. Do not turn your back on the road to watch a cricket match. Do not appear mystified by the intricacies of an engine (even if you are). And never give a member a sloppy salute.

Contrary to general belief, mechanical repairs do not dominate the patrolman's life, for modern cars do not give a great deal of trouble. Up to seventy per cent of breakdowns are caused by electrical faults, and the patrolman hence has to be a sound circuit-tracer. This skill stood one of them in good stead when a driver complained of a curious clicking noise in his car. Nobody else could hear it, but the patrol found the source of the trouble – in the member's electric hearing aid.

Yet, inevitably patrols have some difficulty in keeping abreast with motor car development, since the positioning of the equipment – and the equipment itself – is not standard. An electrical pump, for example, may nowadays be under the bonnet or under the boot. Systems of jacking vary, and the motorist in trouble expects a patrol to know exactly where to look, first time. To keep patrols fully up to date the

Association runs refresher courses at which films of new models are shown and brochures describing new developments circulated.

Above all, the idea of service is impressed upon novice patrols until it becomes part of their own nature. Only thus can the Association's tradition be maintained. That is its most precious heritage; and it is to be respected for insisting that it stays only in the best of hands.

There, I think, one may appropriately leave this story of the men who serve the motoring public and the community at large so admirably. In these hustling days, when 'devil take the hindmost' seems to be the dominant philosophy, the ideals of service and courtesy are becoming lamentably rare. It is all the more refreshing, therefore, to find in the Automobile Association an organisation which bases its approach to the public upon them. I have been a motorist for over a quarter of a century, and always the A A patrol has been to me a symbol of efficient helpfulness. Now that I have been able to investigate more closely the organisation behind the patrol, I shall exchange salutes with even greater affection and respect.

I may not ever have to ask a patrol to help me, say, to trace a missing wombat, pull a boy's head out of a bucket, or extinguish a fire in my kitchen. But his smiling presence will remind me that, while he rides the roads, the civilising virtues will not be entirely submerged in a mass production age. And for that alone it is a privilege to be able publicly to thank both him and the organisation he represents.

IV. ROOM AT THE INN

RAYMOND POSTGATE

Nobody, so far as I can find, has written a scholarly and satisfactory history of inns and hotels, and the accounts in reference books are either unconvincing or non-existent. There is hardly room to write one here. But there are plenty of romantic pictures of the Old English Inn: here is one by a master.

'We dined' (*Boswell is speaking of the year* 1776) 'at an excellent inn at Chapel-house, where Johnson expatiated on the felicity of England in its taverns and inns, and triumphed over the French for not having, in any perfection, the tavern life. There is no private house, (said he) in which people can enjoy themselves so well, as at a capital tavern. Let there be ever so great plenty of good things, ever so much grandeur, ever so much elegance, ever so much desire that everybody should be easy; in the nature of things it cannot be: there must always be some degree of care and anxiety. . . . No man, but a very impudent dog indeed, can as freely command what is in another man's house, as if it were his own. Whereas, at a tavern, there is a general freedom from anxiety. You are sure you are welcome: and the more noise you make, the more trouble you give, the more good things you call for, the welcomer you are. No servants will attend you with the alacrity which waiters do, who are incited by the prospect of an immediate reward in proportion as they please. No, Sir; there is nothing which has yet been contrived by man, by which so much happiness is produced as by a good tavern or inn.'

Johnson's world was London; he left it only to stay with friends, or to visit highly civilised centres where he was sure of finding something like the London inn. If he had been a more extensive traveller,

he would have found a different sort of accommodation. Smollett the
novelist – true, the worst tempered novelist in English history – only
a few years earlier had travelled the same Dover Road that motorists
may use today. He had written:

'Though I was well acquainted with the road to Dover, and made
allowances accordingly, I could not help being chagrined at the bad
accommodation and impudent imposition to which I was exposed.
These I found the more disagreeable, as we were detained a day extra
on the road, in consequence of my wife's being indisposed.

'I need not tell you this is the worst road in England, with respect
to the conveniences of travelling, and must certainly impress foreigners with an unfavourable opinion of the nation in general. The cham-
bers are in general cold and comfortless, the beds paltry, the cookery
execrable, the wine poison, the attendance bad, the publicans insolent,
and the bills extortion. There is not a drop of tolerable malt liquor to
be had from London to Dover.'

Good or bad, however, the old English inn was killed by the railways. (And when I say the 'inn' I include of course the 'hotel'. Hotel
is only an elegant word from the French meaning inn, just as *Ronde de
boeuf Vichy à la Queen's Hotel* means boiled beef and carrots.) Its death
was dramatic enough: the Iron Road, as the contemporary journalists
inflexibly called the railway, spread from county to county. Year by
year the stage coaches were abandoned. The ostlers (picturesque,
even if they were often scoundrels) detached the coach and put it away
in the barn from which it would never be moved again. The horses
(beautiful animals, even if they were overworked and ill treated)
were led off to the knackers. The landlord of the George and Dragon
(even if he was a robber his house probably dated from the middle
ages) resigned himself to living off the half pints of farm labourers.

What took its place? A newly built hotel, in the nearest town, as
close to the station as possible. Generally, it was a square brick building, with sometimes some pretentious 'Gothic' stonework, with gas-
light, with sash windows obscured halfway up by a brownish net on

which its name might be painted in gold paint, and with a number of
bars and rooms curiously labelled: *Saloon*, *Public*, *Private*, *Commercial*, *Smoking*, *Coffee*, or even *Ladies*. It would be named the Station
Hotel, the Railway Hotel, or the Commercial Hotel. The food was
bad; the charges were, on the whole, low. It has no honourable place
in history, but one thing must in fairness be said of the railway hotel
as a class: its sanitary arrangements were usually better than those of
the old country inn. That is a subject which, however unromantic, has
always been among the first thoughts of the motorist.

For fifty years, the last half of the nineteenth century, there was
very little but railway hotels, boarding houses, and a limited number
of expensive caravanserais at the seaside. The country inns had
declined into dispirited beerhouses. But when motorists began to
travel along the roads in the first years of this century they looked for
meals and sometimes for beds along the old roads, away from the
railway stations. The second question which they asked a local in-
formant was 'And, supposing that I am not caught in a police trap,
what is the best place to spend the night?'

The answer was probably pretty inadequate. The early road scout
had not much information or much judgment; if he had had either, his
answer would probably have been 'All the inns, sir, are intolerably
bad', which would have been no help.

That such an answer is no longer true is due to some extent to the
A A. The Association, ever since 1909, has been trying to answer the
question put by members in goggles and mufflers to patrolmen in put-
tees on bicycles. Originally it only required that the hotel should provide lunch and show a bulletin board, but year by year its answer has
become fuller and more reliable. This colloquy is indeed the basis of
the Association's handbooks, this question and answer between an
Association representative and a motorist who is descending on one
town and then going on to another. Handbook information has never
been primarily addressed to gastronomes who want to know where
suprême de volaille is better cooked than anywhere else, nor to fathers

of families who want to know which are the best beaches for a fortnight's stay. The questions these two groups ask are not unimportant,
and the A A will supply the answers on request: but for the average
motorist the provision of garages, the manners of receptionists, the
cleanliness of baths and bedrooms, the comfort of lounges, the number
of beds available, the hours when the hotel is open, and the absence
of restrictive rules are more immediate matters.

These questions, and questions of prices, have the advantage that
they can be briefly and brutally tested by facts and figures. How lovely
are Slapton Sands? How finely cooked are that roast grouse and this
poached turbot? Matters of opinion! But it is not a matter of opinion
if there is only one bath in the house, if there is no sitting room except
the bar which closes at ten, if the garage has no lock and is used by a
fish van, and if there are only two lavatories and one of them is a
penny in the slot and smells bad. It is a matter of some historical importance that the A A brazenly asked questions on such points, and
that its 'inquisition' was received with roars of indignation. The roars
go on; but they are muted and uncertain, and the British countryside
is less barbarous because of the Association's down to earth queries.

Its inspectors asked, and still do ask, questions covering a whole
range of such subjects. Is there a lift? Does the chambermaid knock
before coming into the bedroom? How many bathrooms are there,
compared to the number of bedrooms? Are the sheets damp? (They
would go so far, in their relentless way, as to put a mirror down in
between the sheets – if it misted over, then the sheets were damp.) Is
there a night porter? How many cars could get into the garage? Is
the hotel licensed? There are many other questions on the forms that
their inspectors use, but they are all of the same kind. Before the first
world war they were sometimes resented and the answers to them
were pretty unsatisfactory. Between the wars the questions were
tolerated and the answers began to improve; there were sour faces
still among the hotel keepers, but the pressure was working.

It is difficult, even for an historian, to estimate exactly the effect of

the continuous questionings of a half-hundred inspectors comprising
AA officials known as area secretaries and area road managers. It
was less, probably, than the effect of the presence of a half-million
Association members, any one of whom might write to Fanum House
if he was badly treated. If he did so, his letter was invariably (as it
still is) used as the reason for a visit by an inspector.

The second world war gravely lowered hotel standards. The Association, however, did as we all did and tried to believe that very little
had changed. It republished in 1944 an interim hotel list; it tut-tutted
over the fact that prices had begun to go up. Why, hardly more than
half the hotels listed were still content to charge 8s 6d to 11s for bed
and breakfast. Presumably these extortionate charges would come
down when peace was signed. . . . But two years later the grim facts
could not be avoided. In 1939 there had been fifty hotels with five
stars in the handbook and now there were only fifteen; there had been
200 with four and now there were only sixty-four. Moreover, these
figures were provisional; there had as yet – August 1946 – been no
inspection, and the Association was provoked enough by what it
heard to tell the press that hotels were 'not giving the service which
was expected'. The Secretary, indeed, added that hotel managers
sometimes treated their customers with 'haughty disdain'. When inspections were resumed, the facts were found to be even worse than
the Secretary feared. Hotels were reclassified wholesale, and the five
star category vanished, not to be restored until the AA's jubilee year.

Nine years have passed since that nadir. Commandeered hotels
have been vacated, building licences have been abolished, rationing
has ended, luxuries have returned, prices have climbed. That British
hotels are far better only a fool would deny. That they are as good as
they should be only a bigger fool would pretend. That they are as
good as they are is to some extent due to the Association's system of
inspection and grading. When its representative visits an hotel,
whether as a result of a member's complaint or recommendation or
as a routine visit, he does not disclose who he is. Only after he has

PLATE 25

In the early days of motoring
hotel standards
were sometimes low.
The A A eased the path
of the tourist
by appointing such
satisfactory inns as the
'Lion' at Guildford –
the first to show the sign –
and by supplying
toilet cabinets
for the use of members.

Today, when the motorist signs in at an A A hotel, he knows that it has undergone . . .

PLATE 26

. . . an inspection extending from top corridor to wine cellar.

PLATE 27

dined, slept, breakfasted and paid his bill does he visit the manager, show his card, and ask the sort of questions I have mentioned already. The reports that he and his colleagues send in are fascinating reading; they give a portrait of the condition of Britain in any given year from an unusual angle. They are not reports of a guerrilla warfare against hoteliers; if a member, say, has cancelled a booking at the last moment, in an out of the way place where re-letting is impossible, the Association tells him frankly he should pay up and say no more about it. But if the service or accommodation simply will not do, then the hotel must go; the Association's first responsibility is to its members, and not to the hotel keepers. Out of many, here is one example of such a report, unchanged except to make the hotel unrecognisable. The visit was not a routine one, for three members had complained; otherwise it was not exceptional:

'Stayed night, room 3, and am of the opinion that all three complaints had some justification. I had lunch at 1 pm on 26th after asking at twelve noon or a little before if they could give me a meal. Soup, steamed codling or corned beef and salad. Sweet did not appeal to me so asked for cheese and biscuits and coffee (not shown on menu). Four biscuits and a sliver of processed cheese was brought to me on one plate. Coffee was poor. Dinner: soup, chicken and ham pie, sweet. No coffee. Both these meals were served in very small portions. Breakfast: porridge, egg and bacon, and coffee only by asking specially and feeling you were being difficult. Two thin pieces of toast in rack to hold four or five slices. Two tiny dishes, one held three teaspoons of marmalade, the other five to six teaspoons of granulated sugar. Had to ask for more sugar as I had used two spoonfuls on porridge. It was obvious, by the time I had to wait, that waitress had not got easy access to sugar supply. The food position is very bad, just like one of the jokes about bad landladies. It is obvious that the two sisters who run this business are out to make all they can on food.

'The whole place is clean and shining and the two little lounges are warm and comfortable. There is a fine outlook at the back. In addition

K

LATE 28 *Some prefer the economy, mobility and informality of a caravan holiday o the conventional hotel or boarding house.*
They are not forgotten, for the A A publishes special lists of camping sites.

to the usual notices re valuables there is a notice in the bedroom "No Smoking in Bedroom". In bathroom "No baths after 10.30 pm or before 7.30 am". There are no keys to the garage and I was told that it would be locked up at night and unlocked in morning. Told in such a way that it was obvious you would be inconsiderate to ask for your car when garage locked. Bedroom clean but mattress too short. It was five feet ten inches and I had some difficulty. Bedroom, otherwise, in good order. At about 10.45 pm there was a loud banging on one of the bathroom doors and Mrs A, sister of Mrs B, was shouting to occupant to turn the hot water off as it was past 10.30. She made a great deal of noise and had anyone been asleep she would surely have woken them. I was to learn that the person concerned, a R N commander, frequently had a bath at that time, and I think intentionally because of the notice. Likewise there must have been many who smoked in bedrooms, because of the written command and not so much that they wanted to. Before leaving I saw Mrs B and her sister. The latter seems to run the place. I told them of the complaints and they showed me around. All bedrooms were clean. Some of the mattresses were small, including one complained of by a member. It was five feet eight inches to nine inches. I was told that no other residents had complained but that they would be careful whom they put into such rooms. They did not suggest obtaining longer mattresses. The notice re smoking was explained away as a precaution since a fire at the hotel. Notice in bathrooms due to lack of hot water early in morning. The sisters took more notice of my criticisms than of the three members'. Unfortunately they do *not* consider food inadequate and say that if more sugar, toast, etc, is required guests have only to ask. In conclusion, the hotel does rock when heavy trains pass, but this is not often.

'Feel we should now send final warning letter.'

Some inspections have been more dramatic. In one case, the bed was so filthy that the A A man slept on the floor. In another the manageress played practical jokes on the guests. In a third she burst into tears when the inspector suggested one or two improvements were possible. But these aren't normal; the normal picture is – what? It is hard to say. The hotel proprietors complain fiercely of their hard task, blaming their faults mostly on the *Catering Wages Act*. It is true that this prevents them keeping on duty, for example, a hall porter all day without paying him heavy overtime; but I suspect that they often blame the Act for what is merely the result of full employment. Act or no Act, they would not get people to work long hours at minimum rates, any more than other trades can. Nor does the Act press very hardly on large establishments which can rearrange hours, or on quite small ones where the landlady is not too proud to grill a chop or carve a cold joint for a latecomer. It does seem, however, that the scales under the Act are rigid in a way that presses very hardly upon the medium sized hotel, which forms after all the largest class.

However, the Association has to look at the facts impassively and classify hotels accordingly. It has categories of one to five stars, and another separate category, without a star and just called 'approved'. Most people know this; but not everyone knows the meanings of the stars, though they are in the handbooks. Many members, and even more hotel keepers, seem to think that they are measures of quality – that a three star hotel is a better one than a two star, and so on. There are recurrent heartbroken wails from hotel keepers who want to be 'put up one'. This is all nonsense: stars are merely indications of a category. A three star hotel is no more superior to a one star than a large blonde girl is superior to a small brunette. It all depends on what you like. A hotel either has, or it has not, huge lounges and dining rooms and cocktail bars, bathrooms to almost every bedroom, squash courts and a golf course, an army of uniformed servants, a ball-room, and a band playing every merciless night. If it has, and if it is in fact appointed, then it must go into a high category. The Association is not therefore saying that it is the best possible sort of hotel.

Another criticism which is made of the Association's classification of hotels is not so easily disposed of. It is said that it pays little or no attention to the quality of cooking. It obviously watches quantity, as

is shown in the report printed above; it watches cleanliness in the
kitchen with even more lynx-like eyes. But, it is claimed, it makes no
judgments about the cuisine in the strict and gastronomic sense. I am
inclined to agree with this criticism, though perhaps I am a prejudiced
witness. But I don't think that I am: the great majority of English
tourists do care very much about cookery these days.

In fairness, however, it must be admitted that there are at least
three hard reasons why the Association's limitation of itself is inevitable. First, the estimation of the quality of any cuisine is a matter of
opinion – of highly trained, highly paid and frequently tested opinion
at that. It probably couldn't be done at all in this country; it certainly
couldn't be done without great bitterness and justified charges of un-
fairness. Secondly, gastronomy is by no means the first preoccupation
of the visiting motorist, the descendant of the men in goggles and mufflers. The questions on accommodation that the Association already
asks are far more important to him. Thirdly, I should myself add, the
result of imposing such standards would be that in some fairly large
areas the Association would tell its members there was no tolerable
place, and that they must give up the idea of going there. And that,
in most cases, would not be sensible or practical advice at all.

V. ENDLESS JOURNEY

BRYAN MORGAN

Not very long ago one of the AA's area secretaries was faced with the problem of a member who had complained of being overcharged by an appointed garage. It was a complicated situation, but the secretary knew how to cope with it. Ringing for his area road manager, or ARM, he pushed a file across and said simply 'Go out and deal with this one with your usual mixture of tact and cheek'.

The last word must have been merely a synonym for assurance – for, as Stenson Cooke said, the AA neither gives lip nor takes it. But something like these qualities are the essential requirements of the Association's ARMs – of whom there are at present only fourteen, since several cover more than one area. Directly responsible to their local secretaries, they are the travelling eyes and ears and mouths of the motoring public, its instinctive experts in public relations and its front of house managers. It is thanks to the AA's highway patrol – composed of area road managers and the area secretaries themselves – that a thousand jobs are done annually which might otherwise not have been done, or have been done badly, or have been done too late.

But it is not easy to particularise the area road manager's work, which is in fact the work of at least three men. He is, for instance, responsible for inspecting accommodation, and he and his colleagues pay a routine visit to almost all the AA's 4,000 hotels – approved, as well as appointed – in the course of a year. Whether dropping in for a meal or making an overnight stay they must be aware of the noisy cistern, the leaking garage: and whilst not necessarily gastronomes their palates must be cultivated enough to detect the difference between butter and margarine, between mutton and lamb. But they are equally charged with the inspection of the Association's garages, and though again no specialised knowledge is required of them they must be able to assess efficiency and know what charges are reasonable. Finally the area road manager does exactly what his title suggests and keeps an eye on road conditions, traffic difficulties, and sign-posting requirements.

As such, his job is a curious one, a continual weaving to and fro along the highways of Britain. Spending most days and many nights away from his base, he is perpetually in search of changes which may benefit members and non-members alike. Like commercial travellers who are selling nothing but a service, pilgrims for whom the way is its own goal, the area road managers as a corps have no equivalent in any other organisation – private or nationalised, motoring or general – in the world, though the AA has had them since the first world war. The ARM's work has even a quality of timelessness, for to him there is no inconsistency in spending the morning considering how the arrangements for a centuries-old charter fair might be modified to cause less inconvenience to contemporary traffic and the afternoon recommending lighting improvements on a by-pass. He may deal one day with traffic observation at a new roundabout and the next with the complexities of Lord of the Manor rights.

Perhaps one third of the ARM's time is taken up in routine inspections of hotels and garages, and another third in investigating road conditions on his own initiative. But for the remaining third he is dealing with members' suggestions: and the member who for the first time complains that the sheets in his hotel were damp, or asks why the local council does nothing about that dangerous corner at the end of the road, is often surprised when a little later an Association official calls on him with a file of papers showing that much thought has been given to his letter and that either constructive action is being taken or there are good reasons why none can be taken.

In an age of dusty answers and indefinite delays from public authorities, of 'the customer is always wrong' mentality of too many

individuals, the AA thus performs a unique service in making felt the needs of the ordinary, voiceless user of the roads – though it has just as happy relations with residents' associations and the like. It welcomes comments and complaints: it deals with every one with real thoroughness: and it never closes a file until its area road manager has seen the member and explained what has been done.

But the qualities of the ARM are never called into service more than when he is dealing with road conditions: and then, too, he must have a great store of miscellaneous knowledge to draw upon. He must, of course, be acquainted with the Association's general policy in matters such as the best way to guard children crossing a road outside a school or the provision of footpaths alongside roads. He must be enough of a lawyer to keep in touch with ever changing regulations; and he must have the eye, if not the expert equipment, of a surveyor. He must have some detective ability, and a lot more commonsense. And just now and then he must make rather out of the way decisions, such as whether a tree is in danger of falling, whether the slipstreams from aircraft could be prevented from blowing cyclists across a road by London Airport (they were, by the erection of an earth bank), or whether more effective washing of lorries leaving pits of fullers earth might not improve surface conditions.

Yet for all this, of course, the ARM has no executive power and can only *recommend*. If he finds a signpost overgrown by foliage or a badly sited island he can only approach the relevant authority with a case to lay. And so complex is the pattern of Britain's highways, so many county and city and borough and rural district councils – each with its own corporate personality – have a finger in every pie, so many matters have to be worked out by negotiation upwards to the Ministry or downwards to a concern like a bus company, that the very laying of that case calls for a good deal of knowledge. Roundabouts, for instance, have a way of occurring where the territories of three or four separate road authorities meet, and on one stretch of highway only nine miles long the 'cats' eye' studs come under five

PLATE 29 *The constant preparation of signs keeps specialists b*
in a west London workshop as in area offices all over the British Is
But routine schemes are set aside when an emergency develo

A word of service, and a word about service. In the morning the area road manager may be discussing road conditions with a member, and in the evening talking over a hotel prospectus

PLATE 30

In town and country, in summer and winter,
the A R M is out
keeping his watch on the safety and comfort of all road users.

PLATE 31

PLATE 32

*From its earliest years the Association has been
devising and erecting signs to give
information and guidance to travellers.
These are just a selection of historic examples,
some still doing service.*

different controls. In such cases the area road manager has to know
literally every inch of his roads.

Even when the Association itself undertakes signposting work it
has no *carte blanche*, and for every sign it erects as a public service it
must obtain permission from some public authority. This permission,
of course, is usually most willingly given, and in fact many signs are
erected by request. But there has, over the years, been a steady
change in the A A's function here.

In its earliest days – as is mentioned elsewhere – it had to act
where nobody else would act, and examples from this time (and even
from the pre-history of the Motor Union) are still doing service.
That some of them are not as scratched and battered as they might be
is largely due to one bright idea of the Association when small boys
started shying stones at the signs. It then fixed plates below many
signs threatening prosecution for those who defaced them. Few
people were actually prosecuted, but the boys happily aimed for the
small new sign and left the important one unblemished.

Today the value of the A A's work is perhaps more appreciated,
though many route signs are still stolen as souvenirs and one job was
highly unpopular locally – the erecting of forty signs pointing to
Shaw's Corner. All were torn down overnight by certain inhabitants
of Ayot St Lawrence and its environs who had no love of either the

L

playwright or tourist traffic. But legislation has put the main responsibility of making clear the windings of the English road upon local
authorities, and the signs which the Association now erects fall into
three main classes.

Those of the first type say things like LONDON and TO THE
NORTH. These are technically temporary affairs, and are only there
until the authorities instal their own boards. But a good many of
them have proved at least more permanent than a permanent wave.

The second class of sign is the one most commonly associated with
the AA, and deals with foreseeable interruptions to normal traffic
conditions like road repairs or ceremonial occasions. Random extracts
from those records of the Association's signs department showing
numbers erected read almost like a guide to the British way of life:

Trooping the Colour	50
Dairy Exhibition at Olympia	75
Tennis at Wimbledon	105
Proclamation of Coronation	45
Invalid Tricycle Association Rally	43
Ski-jumping on Hampstead Heath	29
International Eisteddfod	73
Durham Miners' Gala	49
UNO Tariff Conference	75
Stevenage Fair	33
Battle of Britain Week	200
Lord Mayor's Show	50
University Rugby Match	120
Christmas Circus and Ice Show	55

These, and the steady work of signposting diversions of various kinds, account for the bulk of the temporary signs produced by the Association in London and many areas – a production which in a busy month may total 10,000 (more than enough signs to reach, laid end to end, from Westminster to Brixton) and which over the year averages nearly 70,000 (enough, laid solidly, to cover Leicester Square). The majority, incidentally, are made by re-spraying boards that are intended to last twenty years: the AA does not let things go to waste.

But more dramatic are signs of the third type – those which are rushed from stock or produced on the spot by the stencils to which every patrolman has access when he has to deal with an unforeseeable emergency. Names like Lynmouth and Canvey recall the importance of these, but quick work by the Association has prevented chaos in many lesser disasters.

The siting of these emergency signs is of course the work of the patrols on the spot, but many others are erected on the recommendations of the area road managers. For the most part this system works smoothly, though there is one famous case on record when a sign had to be put up other than where the Association thought fit. In that case the lamp post selected for a sign to Goodwood races was found to have been previously commandeered by a swarm of bees. Everybody decided hastily that a better situation *might* be found. . . .

There are a dozen other facets of the ARM's continual watch on the roads – roads which he travels to the extent of some 150 miles a day for five days a week. He may be checking that a central white line is visible, or requesting that a hedge be trimmed to improve sight lines, or considering the approach to a ford. He may be keeping an eye open for streets where local councils have erected lamp posts (a Good Thing) but in doing so have automatically imposed an unnecessary 30 mph restriction (a Bad Thing): for dozens of times a year the AA makes a new – and usually successful – move in its historic and never ending battle against unnecessary restrictions. He may have to check a query arising from a route map, or supply information for some new publication. He may have to make a rush call on a burst water main or a collapsed scaffolding, or impress on a local council the importance of building a temporary bridge. He may be asked by a school to advise on the provision of guard rails at its exits. He may spot the need for a whitewashed ring round the trunk of a tree, for an alteration to a road junction which costs only a few pounds and may save a few lives, for a change in the timing of a traffic signal, for the shifting of a telephone kiosk, or for the moving of a zebra crossing so that it is more visible.

At times the problems which reach the ARM have odd solutions. Complaints from suburban residents that their back street was loud with traffic through the night, for instance, were traceable to the fact that a sign on a nearby main road was badly lit and that heavy lorries were taking the wrong turning, whilst in another case continual hooting along one stretch of road was found to be due to the angle of a shop front giving the impression of headlamps approaching from a turning. At other times he may have to wait a long while to get action taken: the installation of a reflector on a dangerous bend or the marking of a kerb in black and white may be put through in a day, but persuading British Railways to build a new signal box which gave the level crossing operator a better view of traffic took many months, and one official has been trying to get something done about an unfortunately situated snack bar for the last ten years.

In yet more cases the area road manager may be giving advice which eventually is embodied in AA campaigning at the highest level. More rational driving signals, clear de-restriction signs, removal of level crossings, free parking facilities, the use of danger signs only when the danger is not obvious and of 'Slow' followed by an indication of the danger in preference to 'Halt' – all these policies have ultimately been formed as a result of the experience of men with an intimate knowledge of road conditions.

The areas entrusted to the ARMs vary widely in extent, and may be as built over as Leeds (where they prefer brisk 'owt' or 'nowt' replies) or as residential as Exeter (where more leisured converse is

PLATE 33

When your small son is deciding
that it is time he was travel sick,
suggest that he count the A A signs
along the roads of Britain.
They are surprisingly
numerous and varied.

Some ancient cities, like Canterbury (above), have kept their medieval planning almost intact.
In others, such as Norwich, there have been highway widenings over the last fifty years, as shown (left) in the two views of the same street corner. Each type presents different signposting problems.

Barrack Street. July 1936

PLATE 34

*Out on the
open road, too,
the motorist
may find obstacles
to progress.
They would
cause him
more delay
were it not for the
work of the A R M.*

PLATE 35

PLATE 36

*The place names
of Britain
are sometimes
surprising.
But the A R M
knows intimately
his local Moscow
and his
county's Canada.*

the rule); but only in two cases do they have very special features. One of these exceptions is Ireland where, until very recently, the Association has been responsible for the great majority of all sign-posting. (Sometimes it has had to make tricky decisions concerning the Gaelic, for one town in Ireland can be spelt in sixty-three ways.) The other special area is London.

In any great city, of course, the area road manager has to turn his attention from the problems of a country highway system inadequate to modern needs to those of narrow congested urban streets. But London presents problems unique in the world, and an official of the Association is especially charged with it. Major schemes like the 'throughroad' and 'ringroad' signposting which was so largely pion-eered by the A A: intermediate ones like re-numbering signs on the approach to the Great North Road: comparatively small ones like improving the parking arrangements on Hampstead Heath or at Wimbledon, or getting unofficial 'No Parking' signs removed: all these are the particular worries of the London experts. In an attempt to throw more light on the traffic problems of the capital the A A has used techniques ranging from an aerial survey to the analysis of tracks in snow, and has suggested schemes for underground parking. But at this level its activities move into the field of parliamentary agitation.

And for the most part the A R M's own life is an unglamorous one, largely spent in observant solitude. Contemplative and lonely that life may be; but the area road manager is usually a man at ease in an itin-erant life of casual contacts, and with twenty different jobs to be dealt with in one day it is rarely dull. Rather, like the landscape of Britain, it undulates forward, ever changing and quietly interesting.

There are perhaps 350 hotels to be visited annually by each A R M as a matter of routine, and fifty others in answer to members' letters or new applications for appointments: there are seventy-five regular calls on garages and as many more special ones. There are occasional attendances at court and watching briefs at inquiries. And there are the highways and traffic inspections, hundreds of them each year,

ranging from simple ones which can be tied up in a minute to those
for which the A R M must wait weeks for the right weather conditions
(a moonless night when the roads are slippery, say) to recur.

Looking for trouble but never inviting it, imbued with an immense
capacity for absorbing rebuffs, at ease with borough surveyors, village
policemen and members with very different backgrounds, in two
senses keeping an eye on the roads and in two senses making the
crooked straight, the area road managers hence work their way in
brief stages across those roads of Britain of which every mile reminds
them of some crisis resolved: and to travel with one of them is to see
those roads through new eyes. The importance of their work is perhaps most appreciated when one remembers that of the 5,000 or so
traffic recommendations which they make annually the great majority
are swiftly and effectively carried out and almost all the small remain-
der are shelved solely on financial grounds.

And that is where a mixture of tact and cheek gets one.

VI. THE BOYS IN THE BACKROOM

BRYAN MORGAN

To find out how it all started one has only to browse through an early H. G. Wells' novel – through *Kipps* for instance, which was published in the very year of the AA's foundation. There you will find the little farrier's shed or cyclist's shop beginning to provide some service for the automobilist, even though its proprietor often believed that petrol and paraffin were synonymous terms. You will find the hotel which realised that the tourist was not a pariah and which might advertise 'Stabling for motor cars. Engineer in attendance'. But you will find, too, the man with a future – the young technician who in some back room was dreaming of such services as a profession in itself.

Even Wells, however, could hardly have envisaged the scene today. The sophisticated smithy still survives in rural backwaters, it is true, but when one thinks 'garage' one thinks more of the great concrete palaces which stand at so many intersections of arterial roads. Neon lit, offering through electric pumps a range of petrols as perplexing as a wine list, they provide along our highways all that the motorist may desire – lubricants liquid and solid, free air, free water, free battery service, festoons of tyres, hoists which go up and down like cinema organs, engineering plant, garaging space, hire cars, all-night service with a smile, pretty girls to wipe your windscreen, waiting rooms, toilets, even restaurants.

Without such places the 1905 enthusiast who loved getting out and getting under (and who in fact might have considered that to ask for expert help was *infra dig*) would never have yielded place to the 1955 AA member who demands only trouble free motoring, who possibly does not care which end is the big end, and who may even have to ask the Association to trace in which garage he left his car. Without them the sport of automobilism would never have developed into the convenience of motoring.

And the A A gave a very helping hand in this development. Three times in history – when it opened a garage to take care of parking problems, when it set up England's first pump filling stations, and when it devised the radio linked night breakdown service – it even poked its finger energetically into the garages' own pie. But on the whole it has believed that the proprietors know their business best: and hence, when it has found it necessary to indulge in a really big gesture, that has been strictly non-profit making and by way of service to the motoring public. The Association has never desired to enter into competition with the garage men, most of whom are in any case private members. And its guidance has generally been exercised through that friendly and unspectacular – but thorough and unceasing – process of the inspection and possible appointment of garages which ask to be inspected and possibly appointed.

This began in 1908, and arose out of those buccaneering days of warning balls on poles which are described elsewhere. After the first world war the 'starring' system for hotels (begotten, it is believed, by Stenson Cooke's meditations on a brandy label and realisation that three stars were an international symbol of good quality at a reasonable price) was applied to garages; and it continued to be applied until 1937, with refinements as the years went by. Today, with a general levelling up of basic standards and a tendency towards specialisation, the garage stars have disappeared; but more detailed information than ever is conveyed in the handbook, and the internal reports of the A A are still based on criteria which (though in fact laid out in considerable detail) may be broadly summarised as 'major', 'adequate' and 'relatively minor' under the headings of 'repairs', 'servicing' and 'bodywork'.

The kind of night breakdown service given, the provision of garaging accommodation, the makes of cars for which the garage is a

PLATE 37

*From the A A's pioneering experiments
with parking places (above, left) and
filling stations (right)
has developed the modern garage,
now serving the motorist by day and night.*

Steering alignment, headlamp adjustment, exhaust gas analysis
and electrical equipment – these are only a few of the things
tested by the vehicle inspection service.

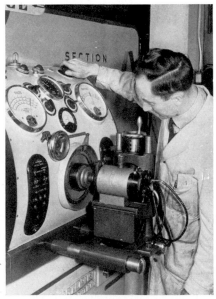

PLATE 38

service agent and whether it handles motor cycles – all these are indicated in the A A's usual laconic style. And if there are members who
would like even more information (about the pretty girls, for instance)
– well, one reason why this cannot always be provided is that
1,500,000 copies of the handbook are distributed free each year, and
the cost of printing alone in inserting a new symbol might run into
many hundreds of pounds.

Before a garage proprietor can receive the Association's 'Yes',
'No' or 'Wait' in answer to his request for appointment, something
like 130 questions must have been answered. As with hotels, with-
drawal of appointment is automatic on change of proprietorship: as
with hotels again, the appointment depends on a balance of absolute
standards and relative local needs. The spirit looked for in the inspecting officers is shown by one quotation from a recent memorandum circulated to them on the subject of bodywork. 'The possession of a
spraying gun and ability to beat out wings,' it says, 'does not merit
classification under this heading.'

'The brakes need fixing.'

So with critical attention the A A examines lathes, welding equipment, drilling and grinding machines, re-boring facilities, salvage apparatus, electrical plant, alignment testers, the quality and quantity of staff, cleanliness and service above all, and even architecture in so far as that can be considered without consigning ninety-five per cent of garages to the outer darkness. It keeps a sharp eye open for such details as whether a mechanic protects a wing against being scratched by his buttons when he bends over it. The reports which are eventually turned in, then, are well considered: but they are only acted on in conjunction with the recommendations of six quite independent members. Experts may fail, and the Association knows it.

Even when a garage is appointed that is far from the end of the matter: for, at the risk of spreading a little despondency, it must now be confessed that motorists are sometimes dissatisfied with the way a job is done or with the money they have to pay for it. In such events, of course, the Association steps in, and in really bad cases sees to it that the offending garage is withdrawn from the handbook. But on the whole its intervention is rather more judicial than when hotel complaints arise. One reason for this is that a decision on what constitutes a satisfactory repair tends to be a matter of hard fact rather than of opinion. Another is that a man who would never report a hotel because he felt poorly after six helpings of welsh rarebit is quite capable of tinkering with the ignition of his engine, reconnecting the leads wrongly, ruining the plates of his battery, hammering at the distributor in frenzy, and then cursing the wretched garage which cannot put things straight in a few moments and for a few shillings.

Just as unreasonable is the motorist who does not get an estimate, or who fails to realise that an inspection following a slight accident may disclose all kinds of 'wear and tear' troubles for which nobody but he can be expected to pay. In such cases the A A can only point out that its members' interests are best served by its maintaining so strict an impartiality that garages, insurance companies and courts are ready to recognise its experts as referees and unofficial arbitrators.

*The A A and 'Punch' agree that
there is little to choose between these scenes.
Efficient garages, they feel,
should look like efficient garages.*

This leads on to the vehicle inspection side of the A A's technical services – a side which has been operating since before the first war and whose activities provide such an index of motoring history that, when the 30 mph speed limit was introduced in the mid-thirties, the Association put a special fleet of vehicles on the road to help members to calibrate their speedometers. The demand for vehicle inspection was heaviest in the post-war period when cars of dubious ancestry were at a premium, but requests still total over 10,000 annually.

The inspections may be carried out either by a van stocked with precision instruments as well as conventional tools, or at the Association's own garage in west London. This latter is probably the only 'A A garage' which does not appreciate a motorist driving in to ask for five gallons of petrol, for it exists mainly to service such of the A A's two thousand and more vehicles as are within easy reach of the capital: but one large department of it is given over to the less portable equipment needed to check members' vehicles. This includes ingenious arrangements of pendulums and prisms which ensure accurate wheel alignment, and a costly maid of all work of a test bench which measures everything from the condition of batteries to the composition of exhaust gases.

The reason for inspection, also, may be one of two. Either a member is dissatisfied with substantial repairs, or he wants an independent verdict on a secondhand car which he is thinking of buying. In either case the result is that a highly qualified engineer – a staff man or a trusted consultant, of whom the Association retains over 150 – does everything to the car short of taking it to pieces. Since there are vendors not above painting a doubtful lily, the results of these inspections are sometimes dramatic: a whole chassis may be eaten away by rust, for instance, since corrosion is the main source of trouble in secondhand cars just as unmatching paintwork calls for most attention in after-repair inspections. But more often the faults which come to light – a missing cotter pin, or a hair crack in a casting – could have been found only by an eye and a mind trained in such detective work.

A car inspection, lasting perhaps four hours, may disclose forty faults ranging from lead-filled rust holes to a chipped battery case. Two hours of writing follow, to produce a report which can run into 1,000 words and which is, as a point of honour, delivered within thirty-six hours of the survey. . . . Six hours of expert time, perhaps the referring of some metallurgical problem to an outside specialist, perhaps a 150 mile journey by the inspection van, perhaps the use of such expensive specialised equipment as few garages can hope to possess – all this is available for a sum ranging between £1 10s and £3 5s. The service is, of course, from the Association's point of view, quite uneconomic: but the Association believes that there is a real need for it, and subsidises it accordingly.

Yet garage and vehicle inspections are by no means the only jobs of the technical men, and their services extend even beyond such matters as chasing difficult spare parts, making routine checks on group members' fleets of vehicles, advising purchasers with difficult requirements, campaigning against noisy motor cycle exhausts or helping members to find chauffeurs and continental couriers. There is, for instance, a close liaison with the legal advisers of the AA; for defects in crankshafts and in contracts tend to go together and the technical executives must themselves be competent lay lawyers.

As an example of this one might take the case of the member who complained that he had been misled over a sale and who produced an impressive looking guarantee. On examination this sheet of foolscap was found to be covered with total gibberish in small print. In another case a motorist was accused of driving 'under the influence' on the grounds that he had zig-zagged wildly across a street. A conviction would have ruined his career; but technical inspection was able to satisfy the lawyers that the fault lay in the driver's steering gear and not his thirst, and a less serious charge was therefore proffered.

Sums ranging up to £300 are quite regularly recovered through the engineers' sixth sense for any hocussing of log books, plates or engine numbers. Yet an even more valuable service was once rendered an overseas visitor who was unfortunate enough to be involved in an accident with a sports car at a T-junction. The fault lay, he claimed, entirely with the driver of the latter vehicle – a young man showing off to his girl, who suffered injuries in the accident. But as soon as the tourist took local legal advice he found that this would be hard to demonstrate, for he himself had no friends or influence in the district whilst the other driver had plenty. . . .

It was then that the A A took a hand, in the form of a genial Scot who held an important position on the technical side. This official went to the scene of the crime and, through a long afternoon, reconstructed what might have happened. He studied the surfaces and the sight lines across hedges; he noted the presence of some road works which must have caused the member to slow to a very modest speed; time and again he drove up to the junction, at different speeds, from different angles, and with different degrees of braking. At the end he was certain that the visitor's driving could not have been dangerous.

And so, armed with this information, the A A paid for the case to be taken to quarter sessions and a jury, and there achieved an absolute discharge for its member.

Even engineers have hearts (they have been known to move heaven
and earth for the return of a deposit to a woman whose husband died
just after he had agreed on a car purchase), and, in the case described
above, their hearts warmed to the idea that they had helped to see
justice done. But if for the most part the work of the technical services is remote from drama, it is none the less valuable for that. The
men who spend much of their lives supine under chassis, and those
other men who work in offices lined with files ranging from 'Alternative Fuels' through 'Lighting Problems' and 'New Car Tests' to
'Winter Motoring', may be the backroom boys of the A A; but it is
through them – through their handling of 100,000 queries annually –
that even the non-technical member is assured of anxiety-free driving.
And that, they think, is largely what the A A is all about.

VII. ROOT AND BRANCH

DAVID KEIR

The first time I visited A A headquarters as editor of this book the sky was a bright blue and the plane trees in Leicester Square were in full leaf. This alone seemed a good omen: and as it turned out no task could have been more engrossing. For the A A – itself an image of the plane tree's sturdy trunk and many branches – was clearly quite as devoted to the motoring cause now as it was in its sapling days. It also had an exciting story to tell.

The moment one walks into the reception room at London's Fanum House there comes a quick sense of a purposeful atmosphere. Round the walls are coloured relief maps with the roads of Britain stretching away to the farthest corners of the island – which are tempting enough. Below them are the receptionists, who always seem more busy than beavers as they deal with members' requests for a route to Thurso or information about motoring conditions in Pernambuco. Less publicly, as I discovered on that first visit, a radio controller in the operations room may be arranging help for a stranded motorist at Putney, since Fanum House is not only a national headquarters but is a branch office for Greater London, just as Fanum Maidstone is a branch office for Kent.

But how did such a far reaching organisation run itself, I wondered? Was it conducted like a big business or a government department; or had it, after fifty years, evolved an individual structure of its own? Let us see.

At the top of the A A is an executive committee consisting of the Chairman, two vice-chairmen, the treasurer and twelve other members. These are honorary appointments made by election: but this could hardly be otherwise, for it has always been regarded as an honour to serve on the AA's supreme governing authority and those who enjoy the privilege do not take their responsibilities lightly. Just as the cabinet of the country is accountable to Parliament, so too the AA's executive committee must give members a regular account of its stewardship at an annual general meeting. Traditionally the committee have been men with wide experience in varied spheres – members of both houses of Parliament, soldiers, sailors, lawyers, engineers, doctors, industrialists and racing drivers. Their combined knowledge has directed the course of policy and change.

Next in status comes the Secretary. As head of the entire staff the Secretary must see to it that the committee's policy is implemented throughout the organisation. He is in fact – and in a very real sense – the permanent official who carries the highest and most continuous responsibility for running the Association from day to day.

Immediately below the Secretary in the administrative structure are those first lieutenants of his, the heads of departments. These officials naturally enjoy considerable authority. They have their own busy staffs to direct, and a never ending flow of problems to deal with from both home and abroad. But they cannot remain too long in their office chairs. For if the overseas relations officer has to attend meetings of the Alliance Internationale de Tourisme, so too the head of the road services must keep himself informed on the spot of new road problems which may have cropped up from the Scottish highlands to the Association's popular outposts in the Channel Islands.

This brings us to one of the most interesting achievements of the AA. Within its flexible structure a harmonious relationship has grown up between root and branch which dates back to those early years in the long struggle for the open road when the first branch offices were established. To give but one example, it was in 1908 that motorists in the west of Scotland sent out the cry 'Come over into Caledonia and help us'. As the cry seemed urgent, Stenson Cooke left London one day, did a day's work at the new Manchester office, and the same night arrived in Glasgow. During the next thirty-six hours he inspected 120 miles of police trapped roads, held a prolonged meeting of sympathisers anxious for a Glasgow office, duly engaged it, secured a telegraphic address and a telephone number, bought the office furniture, and finally visited a chief constable to discuss the sore subject of police traps in the light of what he had seen. Later such urgencies were less; but the branch network grew, and with it the number of area secretaries.

These are very important officials in the organisation. In the A A's jubilee year there were thirty of them, including the head of the Paris office, and together with headquarters they controlled forty-six area offices, sub-offices, port offices and offices at airports. In addition there are, of course, the mobile offices. There are the shipboard offices, set up every time a port officer crosses the Channel on duty, and the en-quiry offices at exhibitions. Then there are the emergency headquar-ters which have to be established to deal with sudden catastrophes. And, in a sense, every patrolman with information leaflets in his side-car and a good tongue in his head constitutes a one man mobile office.

But these are outside the general structure of the A A's decentralis-ation, with its independent staffs and area secretaries. Responsible directly to the Secretary in London, the area secretary none the less enjoys a generous measure of authority at the steering wheel of his own administration. His status is rather like that of a commander in the field, who has frequently to act on his own initiative – during floods or landslides for instance – without departing from the general strategy laid down by high command.

The offices which the area secretaries run are to some extent replicas of Fanum London. Some of the larger house a staff of at least a hundred; others may have less than a dozen. But whatever their size, the range of activity and the responsibility of these pocket Fanums are equally great. Each carries, for instance, a full stock of home touring routes and maps. (There is one exception to this: Irish itineraries are only prepared at the London office or the offices in

Ireland itself.) They are in control of their local road and appointment services. They are being steadily supplied with the radio patrol and radio controlled breakdown services, which inevitably had to start first in the conglomerate London district. They arrange for legal defence in their local courts of summary jurisdiction, except on charges of an unusual or important kind which might go to higher courts. And they have information bureaux capable of dealing with such queries as 'Where can I study early Chinese ceramics?' – though when it comes to such posers as 'My wife is expecting a baby and has a violent desire to see a field of lavender' they may have to ask London.

Obviously, then, there is a near equality of function among these many Fanum Houses. But if their duties are similar, so too are their privileges and their hazards. There was certainly no wartime distinction between them – or between root and branch – when Fanum Bristol was demolished by enemy bombs, Fanum Southampton seriously blasted, and Fanum London damaged by a land mine. Fanums Cardiff, Exeter, and Liverpool also had their scars; Fanum Birmingham was hit by incendiaries; and Fanum Leeds caught fire.

There surely could have been no harder test of loyalties, nor one with a more lasting effect. For the very fact that it was triumphantly passed not only proved that headquarters and its outposts could together stand the strain of a grave emergency, but has since been a splendid reminder of that *esprit de corps* which seems to animate the AA in days of peace no less than in those of war.

VIII. ANY QUESTIONS?

COURTENAY EDWARDS AND L. H. CADE

In a big, brightly lit, horseshoe shaped room high above the swirling traffic of London's Leicester Square, lights are flashing and bells are busily ringing.

A dozen men are talking quietly into telephones while they flick through books of reference or read from notes, and we are listening in while the world's greatest motoring organisation feeds its one and a half million members with facts, figures and guidance on a million and one subjects. As we stand listening, a member rings Whitehall 1200 to say he has run out of petrol at Putney and could the A A bring him some; another asks the best way to get from Reading to Aberdeen; a third wonders who won the 3.30 and yet another wants to know if they play rugby in Heidelberg. And so it goes on, hour after hour, day and night, as calls come in at an average of one a minute throughout the twenty-four hours.

Most of these naturally relate to motoring and may be referred to the appropriate departments. They are from members who have broken down on the road, who want a solicitor to defend them in court, who would like to know if it is going to be foggy, or who are seeking advice on how to get more miles per gallon out of the family car. The A A takes this kind of question in its stride, and always has done, not only in London but also at its many area offices. But what about the kind of member who rings up, as one did not long ago, and asks 'Can you tell me, please, the name of a west end firm which sells cinema organs?'

When members started asking that sort of question it was a challenge the A A immediately accepted. It could, of course, easily have

said 'Sorry, sir, but that's nothing to do with motoring'. But instead
it set up a special information bureau with a library and an elaborate
filing system to take some of the pressure off the service departments.
However, when members kept asking such questions as 'What did
the Irish republican flag used in the 1916 rebellion look like?' it
wisely decided to stop trying to outdo the British Museum as a repos-
itory of general information and concentrated on compiling lists of
people, bodies and institutions who could be contacted at any time and
who could give informed answers to a bewildering variety of questions. (Offhand, for instance, do *you* know the name of a shipping
company prepared to undertake whaling expeditions?)

Before probing a little more deeply into this fascinating subject of
motorists' thirst for knowledge, and the bewildering variety of their
conundrums, let us take another quick look at the Association's 'bread
and butter' questions. The nature of these varies with the season,
though an unexpected event – the 1953 petrol strike, for instance –
may upset all calculations. There was certainly one winter when the
weather was so severe, and the calls from members to Fanum House
so overwhelming, that the fuses in the Whitehall telephone exchange
blew. But in general, during the summer months, most of the calls are
for mechanical first aid following breakdown and for touring facilities; in winter the members' enquiries mainly relate to normal
services, weather, and road conditions.

All this is routine work. So, to a lesser extent, are enquiries relating
to national sporting events like the Derby, Wimbledon, the Boat
Race and Test Matches. All bring their quota of questions from members who want to know how these great sporting events are progress-
ing. For instance, if Hutton or Compton has an overnight score short
of the century dozens of members may ring up the next morning to
discover whether the magic total has been reached.

The Association willingly answers such questions, believing that
anything of interest to a member comes within its scope. For example, a north London member enquired about the nearest point where

he could collect *Cladonia Rangiferina*. The reply was given within a few minutes. The Automobile Association didn't know, but it knew where to find out. It seems that *CR* (commonly known as reindeer moss) is a kind of lichen that often grows on sandy commons in the Aldershot area and is usually at home in hilly country where heather abounds. But the A A wasn't satisfied with that. It also told its member that further information was available at the Cryptogamic Herbarium at the Natural History Museum in South Kensington. And now we ourselves have a good mind to ring the A A to see if we've spelt Cladonia what-is-it correctly.

There was, surely, a spot of romance in the two pronged query from the member who asked what hotel facilities there were at Gretna Green and whether any regular air service connected with it from Bournemouth; but less happy was the frantic member who telephoned in the small hours to say that he had raging toothache and where, please, could he find a dentist. We like to think that the A A was able to put the poor man out of his suffering. But from now on we feel so breathless that we can do little more than list a few posers.

Ever heard of anybody with size forty-three shoes? We haven't, but the A A was asked what the English equivalent was to a continental size forty-three.

'What,' asked a member, 'is the best powder to take with me to deal with vermin in the Balkan states?' We never learned what the answer to that one was. Could it have been gunpowder?

Neither do we know what the A A replied to the gentleman who asked if he should wear a sun helmet in the Canary Isles. We think it all depends. If you're yellow, you can't take it.

Futuristic was the member who asked the dimensions of a building suitable for housing a helicopter. But that question was no harder to answer than the SOS from a couple who had come to town on business. Where, they asked, can we park our two year old baby?

And here is a nice little trio of questions submitted to the Dublin office: Can you tell me if there are any difficulties in taking a young donkey to England? I have to make a continental trip but my wife is expecting a child, so can you give me the addresses of maternity hospitals in all the cities on our route? I've just returned from the continent but I've left my dentures in a hotel at Lisieux. Can you help me to recover them?

Other seekers – but for atmosphere this time – were the members who wanted a hotel with a literary atmosphere where they could go and write a book, or who sought a town on the English south coast which would give the impression of a French Riviera resort as portrayed on the films.

The A A was once asked by a member where he could buy a weasel, but he was not referring to the kind that go 'pop!' What he really wanted was an amphibious vehicle for use in his mines in South Africa. In another sphere, we hate to think that it was anything to do with motoring when an enquirer wanted to know where he could buy some Pittosporum, for this is a foliage used in making wreaths.

These are just a selection from the enormous log of questions and answers filed by the Automobile Association, and we hasten to point out that we are mere frivolous recorders. For our own part we don't want to know where we can go seal shooting off the English coast or whether Liverpool is west of Edinburgh. Nor are we likely to worry the A A with the poser that recently arrived in a letter from Venezuela, which asked where the writer could buy a sheepskin coat for his wife who was on a visit to Scotland. What, you may legitimately ask, did the Association do about that one? It passed on the enquiry to a well known Oxford Street store which specialises in sheepskins and which eventually sent a coat to Scotland on approval.

Which reminds us – and we risk offending our Scottish friends here – that an American member recently rang up to ask 'Are passports necessary for a visit to Scotland?' Both of us, as motoring correspondents, know from long experience that the A A answers even that kind of question with superb tact, as it did the complementary query from a German who wanted to know if it was safe to motor in

England unarmed. But its sources of information are even more important than the tone of its reply when asked 'What is the mean average temperature during the month of August at Biarritz?', or when it gets the query 'I usually feed my dog on a certain brand of biscuits. Are these obtainable in France?' And it needs to do quite a bit of digging among its own archives when asked 'Can you please tell me the cost of running a car from London to India?'

Some of the questions we fire at the A A ourselves, as newspaper men with editions to catch, must be very tricky at times. But our informants never show any sign of evasion or prevarication – even though some of our press queries must seem as peculiar to them as that of the tourist who once asked the speed in knots of the River Rhine at Godesberg, or of the plaintive agricultural member up from the country who telephoned Whitehall 1200 the other day and said 'Here I am, a farmer in the middle of London. Where can I find the cattle market?'

You could almost say, indeed, that the real meaning of those magic letters 'A A' is either 'Authentic Advice' or 'Answers to Anything'.

IX. THE AA REPORTS

BRYAN MORGAN

The AA is a very British institution: and it has a very British attitude to the climate. When it talks about weather, it means bad weather.

But to the men who work in the information centre of London's Fanum House, fogs and floods and freezes are more than things which make them late home from work. And since man's degree of control over such hazards is small, the Association does the next best thing and reports upon them.

So thoroughly does it organise this work that during the half year from mid-October to mid-April, when weather in the AA sense is anticipated, a map of Britain is the most conspicuous feature of the operations room; and the staff who through the summer months have been answering queries about where the warmest bathing beaches are to be found are now standing by for news of snow, ice, fog and other obstacles to progress. It is, indeed, the full time task of one man simply to chart the ever changing picture of Britain's weather. But, for all that, the AA road-weather service begins not with the staff in a warm office but with the hardy patrolman on the road.

This must be so, since the information which the service passes to members – and non-members, too – must be guaranteed at the start by a trained observer, one who knows the difference between slippery and powdery snow, who can accurately estimate visibility in fogs, and who, above all, will be on the spot to report 'all clear'. If an anxious motorist tells the Association that there is an impassable snowdrift outside his front door he is politely thanked: but if the information is news to the AA (which is unlikely) it is confirmed through the local patrolman before it is handed on.

Yet even before the patrols are on the road the first news of the day's weather will have been received in Leicester Square, since two hours before the night staff there go off duty at 8.30 am reports will have been coming in from area offices with their own emergency staff, from the night breakdown vans, and from patrol officers. These last – known as 'silent hour contacts' – are responsible for seeing that even the loneliest parts of Britain are under constant surveillance. Waking in the small hours to see the silver of moonlight reflected from snow on his bedroom ceiling, or roused by a telephone call from the local policeman reporting fog, the silent hour contact rings round his own trusted informants – farmers, all-night garages, the post office, the bus depot – for news of local conditions to send by teletype to London. By such men a whole underground network of information channels is kept open until the patrolmen are out at full strength in the bitter winter dawn.

Weather, however, is not normally reported directly by the patrols. In order that the facts may be handled with the greatest speed they are reported through a manned 'pivotal point' (usually an A A telephone box) to an area office, from which they are passed on to a report centre. There the news on road conditions for a whole region of Britain is co-ordinated, interchanged with neighbouring regions, and passed in turn to London head office. From there, a brief statement of the national picture is flashed back to the areas. The system sounds complicated, but it is the only way of ensuring that everybody knows what it is essential to know. Furthermore, it has the merit of reducing to a minimum congestion on telephone lines – the main cause of delay at times when lines may be broken by snow, though a cause which is becoming less important as the Association's radio services steadily expand. So seriously does the service take this matter of freeing telephone lines that the incoming and outgoing messages follow different routes across the country.

Hence, as the day staff in Leicester Square smoothly takes over, colour lights are flickering beside telephones. 'A1, all clear,' runs a

message from Brighton: but A1 in this context does not refer to the
Great North road but to a stretch of A21 between Tunbridge Wells
and Hastings, for the service has its own coding system for the identification of the major roads of Britain. 'X14, X15, 25–30 yards,'
specifies Exeter, giving the visibility through fog on the moor,
whilst Glasgow reports 'S5a, snow, rutted; S5b, moderate frozen
snow, dangerous'. As the reports are decoded on to standard forms,
alterations are made on a transparent gridded sheet covering the map
of Britain. And the sign language employed on these is precise; for
the AA has to be thorough in its use of terms, unlike the Glasgow
member who enquired about conditions, was told that visibility was
restricted to thirty yards, but pursued 'Yes, but is there any *fog*?'

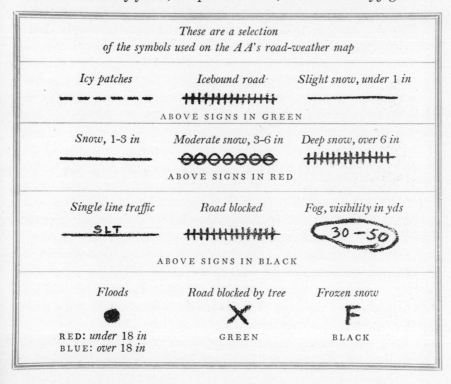

*These are a selection
of the symbols used on the AA's road-weather map*

Icy patches	*Icebound road*	*Slight snow, under 1 in*

ABOVE SIGNS IN GREEN

Snow, 1-3 in	*Moderate snow, 3-6 in*	*Deep snow, over 6 in*

ABOVE SIGNS IN RED

Single line traffic	*Road blocked*	*Fog, visibility in yds*

ABOVE SIGNS IN BLACK

Floods	*Road blocked by tree*	*Frozen snow*
RED: *under 18 in* BLUE: *over 18 in*	GREEN	BLACK

And so, before ten in the morning, a picture of how far abnormal weather conditions may be affecting the highways of Britain is available at Fanum House. Revised throughout the day with information received in the most laconic form possible, and completely re-compiled every week to eliminate any possibility of error, it is in fact the most complete picture available in the country: and reports sent out to the BBC, the news agencies and scores of journals have made the phrase 'The AA reports . . .' almost as familiar an introduction as 'Here is the news. . . .' The Association's latest service to a travelling nation is of course the television weather map, drawn up at six on every evening of bad weather and rushed across London to Lime Grove by courier. This service was introduced in March 1953, on the AA's initiative and largely so that drivers should know which parts of the country they needed further information about and which were clear.

Such releases, however, can indicate only the general pattern of conditions, and the first function of the service is to supply its members with the facts that they require to select a route. When weather is bad – when possibly two dozen major roads are blocked and as many more reduced to single line working – over 4,000 calls a day may be handled in London alone, and as many more in the provinces. The value of the information distributed is shown by the case of the Irish firm which telephoned daily to ask if a certain road was sufficiently free of ice for a heavy boiler to be safely transported and which after a few 'No's' took matters into its own hands, only to find a couple of hours later that its lorry was piled by the roadside and the boiler in a ditch. But there is a lighter side to weather enquiries, too.

There was, for instance, the member who received so gloomy a report on conditions that he just sighed and said 'Right – then I'm staying in bed', and another who thought that the service could tell him at once about the state of the roads in Switzerland. But the most *outré* example of all comes from the west country, where Exeter office was rung one evening by a member in an out of the way village. 'Look,' he said, 'I'm nice and comfortable in the pub here with a pint

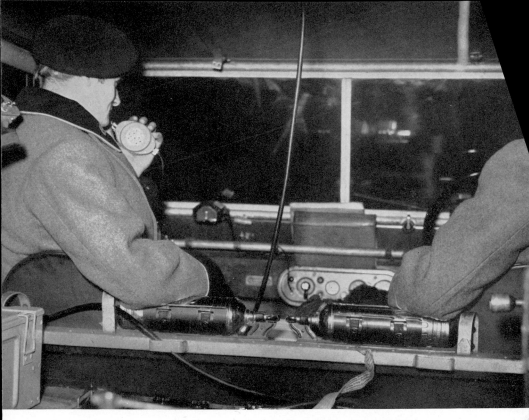

PLATE 39

The technically minded patrol at a radio transmitter, and the farmer working at dawn in districts not normally covered by A A road staff, are alike links in a national network of weather reporting.

PLATE 40

As diverse as the things
one is set to remember
in a party game,
as incongruous as the landscape
of a surrealist painting,
is this selection of objects
which have challenged the wits of the
A A information men (below).

PLATE 41

and a fire. My wife's in Exeter and wants me to take her to a show. So if she rings you up, just be a sport and say that the road's impassable.' The information staff were delivered from a difficult moral problem by the fact that the road really *was* impassable. . . .

The road-weather service has certainly been well tested since after a long prehistory it emerged in the autumn of 1946 as a distinct entity, for it had hardly cut its teeth before that unforgettable post-war winter gripped the country. Power cuts reduced the illumination of the London information centre to kerosene lamps and to candles stuck in bottles; yet under such conditions the Ministry of Food was directed as to which roads remained open and where parcels had to be dropped by parachute on cut-off villages.

Four years later branches not normally open at night worked long hours as fog gave way to chaotic snowfalls, whilst subsequent crises have included the floods of 1952 and 1953 and the great 'smog' descent between them. After this last it was found that only the AA's records of fog distribution were detailed enough to supply the Ministry of Health with vital information: but all such incidents proved the efficiency and value of a service which may need to collate reports from twenty patrols and five offices before it can report 'London to Edinburgh via York, sir? A clear road at three pm'.

Even during what in Britain passes for a good winter, however, the telephones are kept busy with an enquiry every two minutes, whilst, as soon as city fogs begin, a spate of calls from homegoing workers (and sometimes from housewives asking if it is safe to hang out the washing or take the dog for a walk) doubles the frequency. The log of calls is as sensitive a record of climatic changes as a barograph, though the staff who keep it point out politely that some congestion might be relieved if certain members appreciated the limitations of the service. It does not, for instance, forecast the weather; and although the Air Ministry's reports are received directly for the benefit of members twice daily, the Association wisely disclaims responsibility for what the forecasters have to say and could not help a member who asked if

PLATE 42 *Fanum House, Leicester Square, London –*
headquarters of the Association's information services
and of so many other activities.

his road would be clear a week ahead. It does not advise on whether chains or fog masks should be fitted, for conditions are strictly reported 'as at' a certain time and may change radically during a long journey – a point not appreciated by one enquirer who asked if he would be better off in a car or a pony and trap. It will not even advise on whether a journey should be taken at all, for much depends on the skill and hardihood of individual drivers. And when a member enquired about the state of the road between London and Plymouth and, on receiving a depressing answer, asked if it were any better between Plymouth and London – well, the A A felt that there was little to add.

But, with these obvious limitations, the road-weather service remains an invaluable part of the British scene, serving not only members, not only travellers at large, but all the individuals and bodies who need a complete and up to the minute view of the nation's weather. And as such it cannot sleep. Long after a general inter-regional exchange of news at 7.30 pm, long after the stream of incoming calls has died to a steady trickle from long distance drivers and nightclub patrons, the area offices and local contacts are passing news back and forth through the raw winter night, until dawn brings a new batch of reports from the men on the road and a new batch of symbols to be written across the map of Britain.

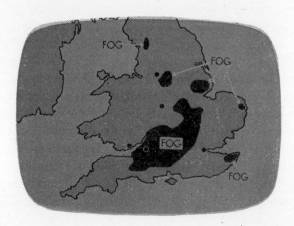

X. ADVOCATES IN ACTION

STEPHEN CROZIER

This member of the Automobile Association was one day not long ago driving his car along a street in which there were also trams. As he had learned to drive in Manchester he was skilled in dealing with this hazard. So when the tram stopped he applied his brakes and waited until all the passengers had descended. But, being of a somewhat dreamy nature, he did not pay sufficient attention and failed to note that a few yards ahead the road narrowed. As he started off again the tram swung to the left, causing him to swerve in that direction too and collide with a cart pulled by a donkey and driven by a female coster of mature years and Italian origin named Anna.

This member (who, though a motorist, is really a very kind man and would not have told the tale in this lighthearted way if anyone had been hurt) was relieved to see that the only damage was to the cart, and that Anna and her donkey were uninjured. But Anna was Latin, and knowing well that there is nothing so devastating to the Anglo-Saxon male as female tears she began to cry. This caused a crowd to collect; for now that women may earn as much as men the sight of one crying in the street is not as common as it was when wives had to wait outside the Red Bull on Friday night to ask their husbands for the housekeeping money and to receive the reply 'Take that'.

The passengers in the tram got out; and the passers by stopped passing by to watch and even to comment, since the spectacle was enhanced by the attraction that this member then had a beard.

'Ought to be ashamed of 'isself. Hitting a little horse and cart.'

'Going fifty miles an hour, 'e were.'

'Fetch a copper.'

Even the tram driver (who was himself a motorist, in an electrical sort of way, and therefore used to being persecuted) looked out of the cab in which he had been twirling levers and said 'They'll do you for this, young fellow. They always do'.

This member, who had read the A A handbook, knew that the wise thing was to say nothing. And for other reasons, which shall appear later, he was well aware that there is no quicker way of making something out of nothing than by talk. He therefore remained silent, and this did not please the crowd.

'Can't even say 'e's sorry.'

'Got a beard 'e 'as – must be one of them Poles.'

'Dangerous driving I call it.'

Some surprise was caused by a little old lady who had been brought up in an old fashioned way, for she said 'Fair play, fair play, the young man wasn't going very fast'. She was shouted down. A few minutes later, when a constable arrived, he caused no surprise to anyone by asking 'What's all this?': and the crowd, most of whom had arrived after the accident, were quick to satisfy his natural curiosity.

' 'it the 'orse and cart 'e did.'

'Dangerous driving.'

'The woman's 'ere, she'll tell you.'

But Anna was not there, having been spirited away towards a cup of tea by a sympathetic housewife. The constable was, therefore, in a difficulty. Having been carefully trained he knew that what crowds say is usually hearsay and that all who wish to become sergeants refer to it as Something Said to Me as a Consequence of Which. The consequence on this occasion was that he began a search for Anna. She being at length found, the constable emerged, having taken down a number of words in English and left out some others in Italian dictated to him by an Anna now fortified by English tea. After the usual preliminaries ('No licence, sir?' – 'All right, I'll produce it at the station'), business began.

'Now, sir, it is my duty to warn you. . . .'

'. . . that I do not need to say anything but that anything I do say will be taken down and may be used in evidence.'

The truth must now be told. This member was once the Police and wore a blue uniform, which he exchanged for a khaki one before complete demoralisation set in and he became a journalist.

The Law was not amused.

'None of that. This isn't a joke.'

'I didn't think it was. I was just helping you out.'

The moving pencil wrote. The member was then allowed to go – which he thankfully did, having smiled apologetically at Anna and taken his hat off to the crowd. This graceful leavetaking, however, drew no courteous response.

'Sauce!'

'Ought to be ashamed of 'isself.'

'Taking 'is 'at orf!'

When this member got home the news was received with some dismay by his wife, as the family were starting on holiday the next day and she supposed that that event would have to be cancelled in order that this member could appear in court. This member, however, knew from experience that it takes far longer than an annual holiday to bring an offender to court for a simple traffic offence, and was able to reassure her on the point. In fact, he was even hopeful that little more might be heard of the matter.

For he knew that the police must serve their summons 'within fourteen days of the offence or serve or send by registered post notice of the intended prosecution within the said fourteen days or the accused person will escape conviction'. As this member had thoughtfully failed to inform the local police station of his holiday address, he thought it probable that the law would be in some difficulty in carrying out the provisions of the Act.

But the law was not to be put off like that. It lay in wait for the lady who came to clean this member's house. And so the letter was eventually delivered to a caravan at Bognor Regis, where this member

o

was enjoying what the travel agents describe as 'a carefree holiday'.

Now this, of course, is the moment when the Automobile Association really comes into the story: for this member realised that if the law would go so far as to lie in wait for his Mrs Mopp it meant business. So he spoke to the legal department of the Automobile Association, which put him in touch with the AA advocate in the town where the 'offence' had taken place.

Accordingly, some days later, this member found himself sitting outside the court on a hard bench in company with some gentlemen who had ceased paying maintenance to their wives without the consent of the court and some ladies who had greeted gentlemen in the street without first being introduced. It was almost an hour after the time indicated for his appearance when he was led in front of the dock.

Then, the formalities having been disposed of and a plea of 'guilty' entered – for this member had undoubtedly been careless – the police were able to make a statement without the necessity of repeating the oath at that regular constabulary rate which even Dr Roger Bannister would have found hard to beat. As this was quite truthful and factual, no evidence was required from the witnesses who were waiting to say on oath:

' 'itting an 'orse and cart',
'Fifty miles an 'our 'e was doing',
'Sauce'

– to a bench which clearly did not appreciate that the accused was a Pole and merely said 'Thank you, officer, that is all I wish to hear'.

The AA advocate was then on his feet; and so deep was his knowledge of the bench, so subtle his reasoning, and so persuasive his words, that this member did not even have his licence endorsed. As he is only a poor journalist he was naturally glad that this effective advocacy had cost him nothing. For the legal service of the Automobile Association is free.

Now, there is a moral for motorists in all this. *If in trouble, ask a policeman. If in trouble with the police, ask the AA.*

There are some cases, like this one, in which the A A legal man can only advise a plea of 'guilty' and leave the bench to fix the penalty. If the case is not serious there is thus engendered an atmosphere of good-will all round. The police are saved the trouble of refreshing their memories from their notebooks; the bench, who have usually heard it all hundreds of times before, are pleased that they haven't once again to examine the plans and listen to the police taking the oath at a hundred miles an hour; and the legal man is delighted that he has been able to surround his client with such an agreeable atmosphere. The result is usually that the member gets a lighter penalty than he would have received had he fought and lost.

But this, of course, is not always so; and many are the cases in which the member has been advised to plead 'not guilty'. It is no easy thing to shake the evidence of the police, but the solicitors briefed by the A A legal department are greatly experienced in motoring matters and are – in a surprisingly large number of cases – able to place a doubt in the mind of the bench as to the infallibility of the police view of a particular incident. The member who wrote a grateful letter to the Association many years ago to say that he believed his case had been dismissed simply because the solicitor defending him knew more about roads, more about motor cars, more about the law, more about the police and more about the bench than any one else in court, has been followed as the Association has grown by thousands of others who have written in the same strain.

For, after all, it is some fifty years since the A A advocates began fighting for members in police courts, appealing from the decisions of the bench, generally taking an aggressive line when the motorist appeared to be receiving less than justice, and sometimes changing motoring law. And it is almost as long since the Association – which, like a medieval knight, had to prove itself in action before it could come to the rescue of others – first entered the lists as the champion of motoring interests.

Most of the cases in the early days of motoring were concerned with prosecutions for exceeding the speed limit, and with the general hostility of the law. The police worked hard for their convictions then. And, as we have seen, they did so by means of the trap, an ingenious device which appealed to everybody (except the motorist) because it was restful and its result was a foregone conclusion.

Earlier in these pages the pleasant way in which the law engaged in this pastime has been described; and there, too, the historic Fairmile case has been explained. But this is perhaps the place to refer to the stopwatch. This instrument the police always had with them in case any member, greatly daring, should demand to see it. But it was not otherwise necessary, since the bench always believed police evidence and never dreamt of asking for proof that the watch was accurate – or even that the police were competent to use it. There was, for instance, the business of that Mr Hearse whose name evidently belied his proclivities and who was charged with exceeding the speed limit. His solicitor suggested, on good grounds, that the inspector responsible for trapping Mr Hearse had thoughtfully arranged for a supply of beer to be sent to him (the inspector) from a local brewery while he sat comfortably behind the bushes. As usual, however, the bench believed the inspector – who stoutly denied these allegations – and Mr Hearse had to pay up.

But whatever the result, there was then such a lack of co-operation between motorist, police and patrolman that only a few years later the chairman of a bench of magistrates could still say 'Motorists have the last right of anyone to be on the road'. And this went on until a driver called William was summoned for driving a motor car in the Bayswater Road at a speed of twenty-five miles an hour – a speed which in those days could be relied on to make horses start between the shafts and the knees of even the most resolute Edwardian gentleman knock beneath his narrow trousers.

Evidence was given by two policemen; and great was the surprise of the bench when William admitted that he had, indeed, been driving just as fast as he could. And then it was that the AA advocate called the owner of the car and the agent of the man who built it to demonstrate to the satisfaction of the court – and of course to the satisfaction of William as well – that it could not possibly be driven at more than twenty miles an hour. The summons was dismissed, and the police retired to think again.

They thought again in a case in which they trapped a man who freely admitted that he had been going very fast. He knew, he said, that Queen Alexandra's car was following behind, and he deliberately put on speed in order not to incommode Her Majesty with the dust that his car was throwing up. 'Nonsense,' said the police at first; but the defendant's story was true, and in due course the charge was dismissed. Even as late as 1931 a member was convicted of driving dangerously on the uncorroborated testimony of a single police officer. The Association appealed to Quarter Sessions, which quashed the conviction with costs against the police.

Times have changed since then. In recent years policemen have spent many weary hours every week checking their motor cycle speedometers over a measured mile, and no bench usually accepts their evidence without calling for corroboration from another constable who has been through the same tedious procedure under the eye and the stopwatch of his sergeant. And for that the motorist has to thank the A A advocates – for they, being erudite and donnish men, realised long before magistrates did that the law could sometimes be mistaken and that even stopwatches made in Switzerland could stop at the wrong moment.

The regulations have been eased in favour of the motorist since those days, and many thousands of cases have been dismissed since over 400 lawyers have been employed in defending the rights of the road user. But the advocates are today busier men than ever. Their cases are varied, and surprisingly often successful. Here are just a few of them.

Many motorists have considered the riddle: 'When is a built up area not a built up area?', but few know the answer. It was provided by an advocate a little while ago, when a member had been accused of exceeding the speed limit on a road in south-east London. The advocate inspected the road on which the trap had been laid and found it was not equipped with street lighting as defined in the appropriate Act of Parliament. Lighting there was: but one post was missing, leaving a gap of 300 yards between two posts instead of the maximum of 200 yards required by law. The summons was therefore dismissed, enquiry disclosing that a bomb had neatly blown up the missing post during the war.

Such pleading may smack of hair splitting, but the fact is that the law of the realm is based on the observance of *minutiae* and that therefore the Association must reason in the same way in order that justice may be done. Hence quite often such a technical spanner is dropped in the prosecution's works. One member, for instance, had failed to produce his driving licence and insurance certificate on demand. In court a police inspector appeared for the prosecution. The advocate rose:

'Your worships, this charge was, I understand, laid by the superintendent of police. He is not in court, and I respectfully submit that in the absence of the actual police official who laid the charge your worships are not entitled to hear anyone but a barrister or solicitor.'

There followed a whispered conversation between the clerk and the bench which resulted in the decision that there would have to be an adjournment; and when the bench added that in such an event the defence would be entitled to costs, the case was withdrawn.

Sometimes a case has to be taken much farther than the police court – as, for instance, in the case of the driver and the passenger who were journeying together along a road in the south of England. The passenger thought he saw a policeman wave at the car to stop. He told the driver what he had seen, and the driver stopped and waited for the policeman, who was riding a pedal cycle, to come up.

'What's this?'

'What's what?'

'You weren't driving just now. The passenger was driving.'

'No.'

The upshot was that the pair in the car were summoned for licence
and insurance offences and that the driver, who was a member, was
fined £20 and had his licence suspended for a year. When the solicitor
reported this to the Association it was decided that the conviction
was against the weight of the evidence, and the case was taken to
appeal, where the decision was reversed with costs against the police.

Any member who works in a town may be under the impression
that the roads belong to the public transport companies and are provided for their sole use, motorists being allowed thereon at their own
risk. It was an AA advocate who exposed the fallacy of that natural
assumption. A number of members had been prosecuted for leaving
their cars near a bus stopping place, the police insisting that obstruction had been caused to the buses. 'No doubt that is so,' said the advocate, 'but can the prosecution produce any evidence of an Order or
other authority granting buses the exclusive use of any part of the
highway?' None could be found, and the cases were dismissed.

Of course, the advocates do not always defend. Sometimes they
prosecute. They did so in the case of a member called Cyril (who was
naturally as inoffensive as a man called Cyril is bound to be) who was
driving his car when he came into collision with a lorry. This latter,
being larger than Cyril's car, had the better of the matter.

'I say,' said Cyril, when he had crawled out of the window of the
car and had dusted himself off, 'you should really look where you
are going. You were on your wrong side, you know.'

'What's that?'

'You were on your wrong side.'

'Not me.'

'You were.'

'You prove it.' It was perhaps at this stage that Cyril realised that
this driver was not typical of his normally courteous kind, for he
then replied:

'I'll report you. I want your name and address.'

'All right.'

These two pictures – 'stills' from a film telling the early story of the A A –

capture the atmosphere of hostility in which the free legal defence service was initiated.

PLATE 43

PLATE 44   *Today, the motorist who finds himself in trouble
is assured of wise, patient and painstaking counsel.*

The lorry driver then got out of his cab and Cyril put his hands in his pockets to look for a pencil and paper. This was unfortunate for him, as it enabled the lorry driver to drop him neatly over the bonnet of his car with a right cross which would have done justice to Mr Joe Louis at his best. But Cyril had memorised the number of the lorry, and in due course an A A advocate supported him in his prosecution of the lorry driver for assault. The fine for this was £1. But the police (who were much more concerned with the driver than with Cyril) charged the lorry man with dangerous driving and with failing to report an accident. For the three offences he was fined £35, and his licence was suspended for five years.

It is not only within the courts that the Association's legal department can help the member. For instance, every month more than £10,000 is recovered through what is known as the claims recovery service. The work of this is highly complicated, and the neon signs of cinemas and restaurants are thus not the only lights which burn late into the night in Leicester Square. In Fanum House, and in lawyers' offices throughout the country, there are learned men thumbing through the pages of learned books. And after they have read them they write letters so persuasive in their terms that even an Inspector of Taxes has been known to dip hurriedly into his official coffers and hand over, to the material betterment of some member.

Briefly, the claims recovery service obtains redress for 'uncovered trouble' – a phrase which anyone but a member will naturally suppose to mean going to Manchester without an umbrella, but which, in fact, refers to cases in which the member has a claim to redress but is not covered by an insurance policy. One such case was that of the schoolboy, the bottle and the member.

The schoolboy was on an outing in a motor coach; and – as everyone who has been down the Brighton road on a Sunday in summer knows – a crate of bottles is as necessary to an outing as that the coach should have wheels. In this case, of course, the crate contained only 'pop', for the passengers were but children. But this schoolboy

P

having drunk his 'pop' recalled – since he, too, had been down the Brighton road on a Sunday – that the adult thing to do on an outing was to throw the bottle out of the window. This he did, thereby causing some surprise and alarm to a member upon whose car it fell, damaging the vehicle not a little.

In vain did the member and his insurance outfit threaten the coach company: in vain did they write letters to the boy's parents. Then the member consulted the Association. The lights burned late, the persuasive words went forth, and it was not long before the member had his car repaired – entirely at the expense of the education authority who had organised the outing. A similar case in which the recovery service obtained redress for a member was that in which the pilot of a helicopter spraying some crops with insecticide mistook a modern black car for a peculiarly large beetle. He promptly sprayed it, to the detriment of its new coat of cellulose.

Not long ago a member took his car to a garage because a core plug in the cylinder block was leaking. The value of a new plug was 4d, and a reasonable estimate of the labour cost in replacing it would have been 2s 6d. The owner was therefore surprised to receive a bill for over £4 for this slight repair. The garage proprietor contended that the plug was so placed that it was necessary to remove half the engine to get at it; but the Association did not find it difficult to persuade him to return the £4 to the member and to convince the proprietor that the game of 'hunt the core plug', if persisted in, was not likely to improve his business.

That is but one instance, and a small one, of the way in which a member was helped in a dispute with a garage proprietor. But sometimes a member finds himself in disagreement with a hotel – as, for instance, in the case when a lady member who was also the mother of a family booked some rooms at a hotel which were (said the management's letter) provided with a view of the sea.

Upon looking out of the windows of the bedrooms the unfortunate lady was, however, unable to see anything but a row of sandhills – a circumstance which naturally caused her alarm and despondency, since she had hoped from the comfort of the room to observe her children and others enjoying the English summer as they emerged shivering and windblown from the water. It is true that her eldest boy, an agile youth, clambered upon the dressing table and was thus able to observe a thin strip of cold grey sea beyond the sandhills: but nobody was satisfied with this, least of all the A A legal department. And in due course certain financial arrangements were agreed with the proprietor of the hotel to the contentment of the member.

In such ways (and they are many) does the legal department serve its members. But, of course, the jobs which the public hears of most are the court cases. And many thousands of these have been conducted by solicitors on behalf of members.

All is not yet well with the motoring laws of Britain: those members who can spare the time from studying summonses and telephoning the legal department to read the newspapers may recall that not long ago a table was published which compared the motoring prosecutions in different cities of similar size and found the average penalties widely disparate. Unfortunate though this is, it may be inevitable, and certainly there is little which the A A can do about it. It has, however, many cards up its sleeve when dealing with a notoriously tough bench. In one case, for instance, an advocate did his best for a member who was otherwise defenceless by making the court laugh when explaining the reason for his client's regrettable lapse from sobriety. The accused had, apparently, been entertained during the day by a printer's agent, who wanted to secure from him a valuable contract. There had been lunch and some business talk. A box of chocolates had been presented to the accused's wife, and the accused himself had been taken and filled up with whisky.

'Your worships,' said the advocate, 'it was a case of –

"Candy is dandy,

But liquor is quicker".'

Who shall say that the fine was not less than it might have been if the advocate had not done the only thing he could do, which was to talk the members of the bench out of the severe state of mind in which they were at first bound to approach the case?

But perhaps it is in bringing about the great change in the attitude of the police and the bench towards motorists over the last fifty years that the legal department has had its finest moments. From the solicitor defending a member accused of a parking offence to the QC fighting for a point of principle in a court of appeal, A A advocates have pleaded eloquently; and in doing so they have not only secured many acquittals but made for a happier atmosphere. The relationship between the Association's servants, its members, and the police has after many years of conflict become one of understanding.

The policeman must report the offending motorist; that is his job. The A A advocate must defend him; that is *his* job. Every member knows that provided he does not break the law the police are there to

aid him, and every policeman knows that the patrols have the same
ambition – to keep traffic running smoothly – and will therefore lend
them a helping hand.

In the war hundreds of civil police fought, and were sometimes
killed, beside patrols of the Automobile Association. Both were serving in the Corps of Royal Military Police. It was the privilege of this
member, who was also a policeman, to command many of these ancient enemies, now friends, who soldiered side by side.

XI. HOLIDAYS AT HOME

CYRIL RAY

There are 186,261 miles of road in Great Britain. 'Almost exactly the speed of light in miles per second,' said a mathematically minded friend who gave me the figures. 'If you travelled at the speed of light, you'd have covered every mile of every road in these islands in less than a second.' I am constantly being overtaken by motorists who are trying to do it.

Inadequate as it is for the volume of traffic it carries, the British web of roads is nevertheless the most tightly woven anywhere in the world. There are two miles of road to every square mile of this country, as against one to every American square mile and (to take a country at least as densely populated as our own) half a mile to each square mile of Belgium.

Up to a point this is an admirable thing. But the more miles of road there are, the more chance there is of going wrong. The English road is traditionally a rolling road, and I haven't noticed that Scottish or Welsh or Irish ones are any straighter. It is possible to take a lot of wrong turnings between Basingstoke, say, and Brighton, or between Doncaster and Dunblane. And on top of this there is the fact that there are more vehicles per mile in this than in any other country, and hence more drivers to take wrong turnings.

The A A, of course, provides tens of thousands of signs each year in an effort to ensure that he who runs may read: but that great work is less my concern here than the service provided for the motorist who premeditates his touring. Well over 2,000 routes a day on an average (less in the winter but more, far more, in the summer) are compiled by the Association for motorists making business journeys, holiday tours, complicated family pilgrimages or a combination of all three within the British Isles.

One rather difficult member might write: 'I want to drive from Epsom to Fleetwood as quickly as possible, but without passing through big towns because my wife is nervous of heavy traffic, calling on an aunt in Bromsgrove and my grandmother in Derby on the way, and then go on for a fortnight's tour of Scotland with a caravan I'm picking up in Blackpool. And could you plan the tour so that I can get in some coarse fishing?'

For a great many years there have been route compilers at Fanum House in London, and at all the area offices, to whom such an enquiry is child's play. Each is armed with *Bartholomew's Gazetteer*, a set of half inch and one inch maps of the British Isles, the Association's own Road Books, an opisometer (the little watch-like gadget which measures mileage on maps) and the Compiler's Guide. This last is an atlas of the roads of the country, arranged as radials from each of thirty or forty key towns and marked as being better for summer or winter driving. But don't ask me where this wonder working guide can be bought. It can't be. It is the A A's own invention: it is the master map from which all routes are compiled: and there are only enough copies for the route compilers themselves. Since you get the essence of it in any route you ask for, and more than the essence in the Road Books, why should you try to buy it anyway?

Sometimes the very place names in the initial enquiry can be stumbling blocks: there are twenty-five places called Overton in the Gazetteer, for instance, thirteen Garths, ten Gatesides and twenty-two Seatons. But granted that there are no problems of that kind to solve, either from internal evidence or by appeal to the member (which Whitchurch does he *mean*?), a straightforward route is almost so easy for the compiler as to be a bore.

There are more than 7,000 standard printed route sections, filed in indexed pigeon holes, that can be fitted together like pieces of a boy's Meccano set to get you from London, say, to Liverpool; what the

compilers like to tackle is something that represents more of a challenge than that. And so I fancy there are times (though not Bank
Holiday times, when applications arrive in tens of thousands) when
they would be glad of some such poser as that devised by James
Fisher, the ornithologist.

Mr Fisher would like to start at Quarter House in Stirlingshire and
then travel, by way of Thirdpart in Fife, to Halfmorton in Dumfries-
shire, thus keeping the fractions in their proper place. After that he
would start the integers in Ireland at One Man's Pass in Donegal.
From Twopothouse in Cork he would return to either a Dorsetshire
or a Sussex Three Legged Cross; and suddenly, he says, one would be
unable to see the wood for the trees. Shall it be Four Elms in Kent or
one of the widespread Four Ashes or Four Oaks? No: he would plump
for Four Hole Cross in Cornwall and travel overseas – with Fivepenny
Borve on the island of Lewis as a stepping stone – to Sixtowns, Lon-
donderry, closing his ears to the tempting peal of Six Bells, Mon-
mouth. Then Sevenoaks in Kent, Eightlands in Yorkshire, Ninestane
Rig in Roxburghshire (had it not been time for another look at Scotland he would have said Nine Ladies in Derbyshire) and double
figures with Ten Acre Street in Worcestershire, Eleven Lane Ends in
Armagh and the Twelve Pins in Galway (whose Twelve Heads, for
some peculiar reason, are in Cornwall). Perhaps we should leave it
there; for though Baker's Dozen is tempting one could go on filling
in every figure up to Yorkshire's Eight and Forty, or Radnorshire's
Hundred House.

PLATE 45

*The change
which the use of
the motor vehicle
for business
and pleasure*
has brought to the streets of Britain is emphasised by these

*'then and now'
photographs of
Bond Street,
London (above)
and The High,
Oxford (below).*

PLATE 46

When the by-roads of Britain
were dusty unmetalled tracks,
the touring motorist
was still tempted to
explore them (above).
He was tempted overseas,
too, even in those days
when his petrol tank
had to be drained dry
before his car
was slung aboard.

But as it is, the compiler must congratulate himself if an enquiry mentions, for instance, that the journey is to be undertaken on a Sunday or in the small hours of the morning: the route can then be adjusted to take the motorist through deserted city streets that would be maddeningly congested in the middle of a weekday, and so save miles on a long run. Or the compiler may have the pleasure of comparing the date given for the journey with a list of special events on his desk, and so route a busy businessman engaged on an important selling tour away from the racecourse or Goose Fair upon which pleasure seekers are converging.

This, of course, is very clever of the A A: but in fairness it must be stated that it did not *invent* the road map. As a matter of fact there have been a good many such since a certain Antoninus in the time of the Emperor Hadrian, 1,800 years ago, produced an *Itinerarium* of the Roman Empire with fifteen journeys in Britain passing through no fewer than 113 towns. The chief journey, by the way, began at Richborough in Kent, the usual landing place from the continent in those times, passed through London, St Albans, Daventry and Manchester, continued over to York and Catterick and then went on to Carlisle and the western end of the Roman wall. More than 500 miles long, it contained (in their Latin form, of course) the names of thirty-seven towns. As an eighteenth century commentator observes, this is 'a curious proof of the flourishing state of population in this our native country, when little more of it than its name was known among the neighbouring nations'.

Once the Romans had gone, movement declined and the roads decayed. It is many hundreds of years before Britain seems to stir again – to stir enough, anyway, for us to hear of royal progresses and pilgrimages, of great lords visiting their scattered estates, of judges on circuit and of the waggon trains of the cloth weavers creaking and lumbering to the ports. The crusades did something to encourage map making and route finding, but it is not until the middle of the sixteenth century that we get another 'itinerary' of Britain to match that of Antoninus – the one which John Leland made for King Henry VIII.

With this second of the Tudors there opened a period rich in those new fangled things, road books. Other topographers, like Harrison and Camden, followed suit, but my own favourite is that of John Ogilby, cosmographer to Charles II and (an odd combination with cosmography) Master of His Majesty's Revels in the Kingdom of Ireland.

Pages from this work and (more frequently) from its various descendants can sometimes be seen framed in the halls of country hotels. Each page consists of an unwound scroll up which runs this road or that, brown with hills, green with trees, dotted with villages and marked, here and there, by some such landmark as 'brook, with stone bridge'. Ogilby, who was himself a tremendous traveller, mapped and engraved 40,000 miles of road 'To Improve Our Commerce and Correspondency at Home, by Registring and Illustrating Your Majesty's High-Ways, Directly and Transversly, as from Shore to Shore, so to the Prescrib'd Limits of the Circumambient Ocean, from this Great Emporium and Prime Center of the Kingdom, Your Royal Metropolis'. In so doing, he not only made one of the handsomest books of maps ever to be produced in Britain, but hit upon all kinds of devices still in use. The strip maps of the AA itself, for instance (and it has been using the system since 1931), though neither coloured nor so prettily embellished as Ogilby's, are nevertheless drawn on the same principle. You read the map up the page, the compass rose correcting your assumption that the top is always north.

With all that has happened on, and to, the roads of Britain between Ogilby's time and ours, there has been no need to abandon his actual method of mapping a route, though the Association naturally makes frequent minor improvements in it. The main difference – and it is the kind of difference that one does not expect – is that the seventeenth century compiler made one set of eighty-five routes that had to serve everybody, whatever his exact requirements; now, in our modern mass production age, you can have your route hand made, so to speak, and made to measure. Much else may have been better then than now, but never before our own time could one have one's route specially prepared, with perhaps even that very morning's information taken into consideration in the event of a flood having carried away a bridge, or a landslide having engulfed a road.

And, speaking of such unpleasant events, how about those awkward loads behind which I always seem to be travelling? How about that caravan that was to be picked up at Blackpool? There are key maps to which the route compilers refer which show the roads throughout the British Isles that are too steep or too sharply cornered for caravans, just as there are sets of maps with the heights of every bridge recorded. It doesn't matter how big the piece of machinery you want to send by road: the AA can suggest a route for you.

However, it isn't only the people who move caravans or vast chunks of machinery about the country who have cause to be grateful to the

*The first of many A A touring publications
was this town plan of Brighton, issued in 1912.*

A A for its knowledge of bridge heights. Not long ago the Association had to map out a route for three giraffes, originally from Nairobi, which had to be taken from quarantine in London to the Chester Zoo. And giraffes come twenty feet high or so.

Perhaps I digress, but why shouldn't I? It is better to travel hopefully than to arrive, though this is not a point I would wish to labour with the route compilers I have been talking about. They have been known to deal competently with motorists wanting a route that would take them through the best country for picking cob nuts, blackberries or mushrooms. 'The road with the best pubs' was one simple request, and easier to answer than another for 'somewhere where the sun's shining'. An American mortician wanted to tour England's cemeteries, and the owner of a steam roller demanded a route where he could fill up with water every five miles. The man who needed a route from Land's End to John o' Groats that would be grass verged all the way was – as one might guess – a horseman. But he was a member of the A A, and as much entitled to information relating to his one hungry horse as I am for my Morris Minor's eight horses.

The home touring service could have told the imaginary member whose imaginary letter I quoted at the beginning of this article not only the roads suitable for a caravan but where he could hire or buy one, where he could park it and where pitch a tent. For whether you are combining a business trip with a pleasure tour, or making a special study of country houses open to the public, or shipping your car by sea to Aberdeen, or sending it by train to Edinburgh, the compilers fill in a slip of paper with neat hieroglyphics; deft fingers reach into this drawer or that pigeon hole; and there it all is, stapled inside a neat buff cover, labelled 'Route prepared as requested' and with the distance (to the nearest quarter of a mile) printed on it automatically.

My own most recent route – 1,568¼ miles of a tour of Scotland from London and back again – was turned out in less than ten minutes and handed to me (as it would have been to any other member) along with the A A's timetable and price list of the Scottish ferries and three

PLATE 47 *Warm Wessex villages like Corfe, little guarded harbours like Stonehaven. .*
It is attractions like these which tempt many to call
the A A home touring service when planning a holida

PLATE 48   *The beauties of Ireland (above) and Wales (below) call many. These many, in turn, call the A A.*

"WHAT ARE YOU GRUMBLING ABOUT? YOU CAME OUT TO SMELL THE
HAY, DIDN'T YOU?"

Through the years, Mr Punch has noted that
home touring may present its particular problems.

From the Roman road book
of Antoninus (left),
through the somewhat
imaginative maps
of medieval England (below)
and the increasing accuracy of such
seventeenth century cartographers
as Ogilby (opposite),
derives the modern
route sheet (opposite, inset).

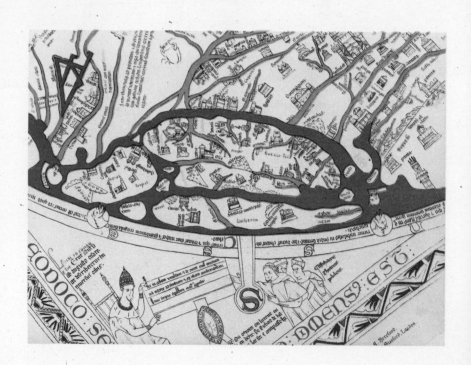

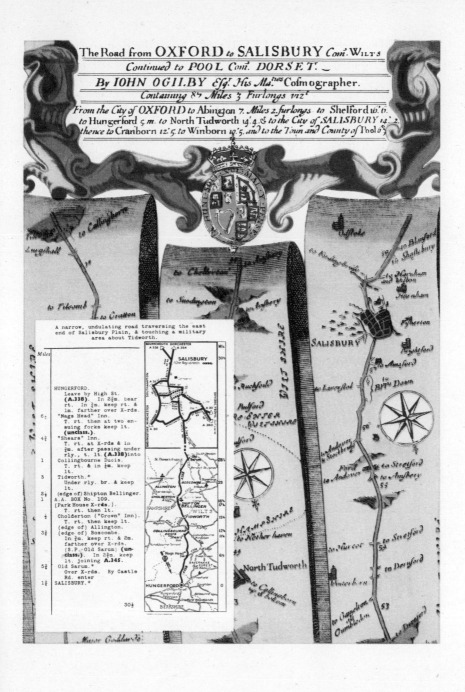

The Road from OXFORD to SALISBURY Com. WILTS

Continued to POOL Com. DORSET.

By IOHN OGILBY Esq.r His Ma.ties Cosmographer.

Containing 87 Miles 3 Furlongs viz.t

From the City of OXFORD to Abington 7. Miles 2. furlongs. to Shelford w.ch 6.
to Hungerford 5. m. to North Tudworth 14.4. & to the City of SALISBURY 14.2.
thence to Cranborn 12.5. to Winborn 10.5. and to the Town and County of Pool 6.3

A narrow, undulating road traversing the east
end of Salisbury Plain, & touching a military
area about Tidworth.

HUNGERFORD.
Leave by High St.
(A.338). In 2¾m. bear
rt. In ¾m. keep rt. &
1m. farther over X-rds.
"Nags Head" Inn.
T. rt. then at two en-
suing forks keep lt.
(unclass.).
"Shears" Inn.
T. rt. at X-rds & in
¾m. after passing under
rly., t. lt. **(A.338)** into
Collingbourne Ducis.
T. rt. & in ½m. keep
lt.
Tidworth.*
Under rly. br. & keep
lt.
(edge of) Shipton Bellinger.
A.A. BOX No. 109.
(Park House X-rds.).
T. rt. then lt.
Cholderton ("Crown" Inn).
T. rt. then keep lt.
(edge of) Allington.
(edge of) Boscombe.
In ¾m. keep rt. & 2m.
farther over X-rds.
(S.P. Old Sarum) **(unclass.).** In 2¾m. keep
lt. joining **A.345.**
Old Sarum.*
Over X-rds. By Castle
Rd. enter
SALISBURY.*

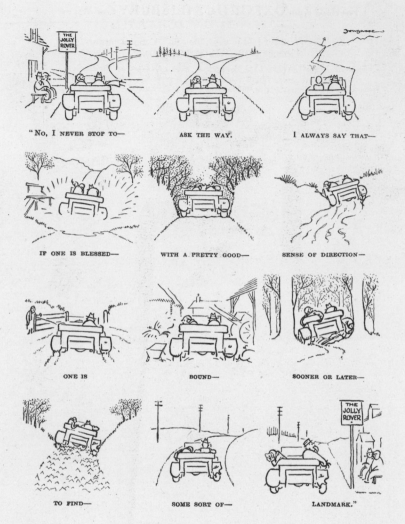

"No, I never stop to— · Ask the way. · I always say that—

If one is blessed— · With a pretty good— · Sense of direction—

One is · Bound— · Sooner or later—

To find— · Some sort of— · Landmark."

PLATE 49   *Even the haunted*
Western Isles
of Scotland (above)
hold few mysteries
for those
who compile routes
and edit road books (left).

handsomely illustrated booklet guides to central Scotland, the low-
lands and the highlands. Another of the Association's pamphlets lists
not only caravan and camp sites but also farmhouse accommodation –
and includes an atlas of the places listed.

But not every member asks the A A for a ready made route or tour.
To some people half the fun of a holiday jaunt is to work it out before-
hand from maps and guides. I am myself lazy in this, as in other matters; but my wife, for one, can use the Road Book to get us from
Baldock in Hertfordshire to Wigwig in Shropshire before you could
say 'National Health Service'. Indeed, I think sometimes that she is
happier in an armchair at home, surrounded by maps, than in the car
I am driving along the very route she has planned.

The Road Books of England and Wales and of Scotland are the
noblest of supplements to the Touring Guide (with its maps and
mileages) and the Annual Handbook (with its lists of garages and
hotels). There is also a handbook for Ireland – bound in green, as
against the yellow one which deals with the rest of the British Isles,
but in fact covering the Orange counties too – and there are plans
afoot for a new edition of the Road Book of Ireland. Meanwhile,
in a recent year the Association provided the necessary documents for more than 26,000 members visiting the Republic. One-
third of these came from across the sea, but to help the other 17,000 or
so with customs formalities the Association maintained a special staff
of frontier officers. Very nearly as many northern and southern Irish-
men availed themselves of the Association's services in Belfast, Dublin and Cork to come the other way.

Every one of the 26,000 members received from the Association a
leaflet of shipping information, a pamphlet guide to Ireland, and a
coloured map on the scale of sixteen miles to the inch with town
plans. There is even a handout telling you how to set about importing
your car free into the south if you move there to live; and I was
delighted to realise, from its quotation of Section 17 of the Republic's
Finance Act of 1936, what the prose style of the Irish civil service

LATE 50 *Across the narrow seas and home to haven under the white cliffs of Dover,*
,800 vehicles may pass on a single day of high summer.
The majority of these are the responsibility of the A A port staff.

owes to its English predecessors in such happy phrases as: 'otherwise than as stock in trade, or as manufactured or partly manufactured stock in trade, or as material, ingredient, or component part for the manufacture of stock in trade'.

After this it is a relief to be told in the guide that there is an abundance of good fishing for sea trout throughout Ireland, most of it free, or that the reason for the proud name of 'Royal Meath' is that on the nearby Hill of Tara once stood the palaces of the Kings of Ireland. Similar information, of course, is there in plenty in the English and Scottish Road Books.

But then, road books and maps are of the very stuff of travel. And for those who use them – if I may quote Byron's *Don Juan* –

'The greater is the pleasure of arriving
At the great end of travel, which is driving.'

XII. AA PLUS GB

HOWARD MARSHALL

Though traditionally the world's greatest travellers, we British have never really overcome our native suspicion that the habits of foreigners were deliberately invented for our confusion. Foreign travel, therefore, has from the earliest times called for a particular attitude of mind on the part of the Briton abroad – an attitude which will protect him against what he supposes to be the general unpredictability of foreigners and their particular failure in a crisis to understand the simplest explanation in plain English.

With the invention of the internal combustion engine our neighbours across the Channel laid yet another trap for the unwary by imposing well nigh insuperable restrictions on the import and movement of motor cars. They were not alone in this: the British customs were – and are – in no way more lenient. But by the time the British motoring organisations turned their attention to the matter (and let me say that they were admirably quick off the mark) there existed throughout the continent a strictly supervised system of deterrents. Briefly, these operated as follows: the motorist, on arriving at his port of disembarkation, had to pay a duty equivalent to one sovereign sterling per hundredweight, plus a deposit – which he could recover on his way back – big enough to dissuade him from selling his vehicle while in the country. Quite apart from the expense entailed, the handful of British motorists who ventured to put the system to the test unassisted by any motoring organisation found it choked with red tape and fraught with frustrations of all kinds. For the moment, foreign motor touring was less a pleasure than an ordeal.

It was in 1907 that the AA determined to make foreign touring possible by the many. It knew that, by using documents called *trip-tyques* and *carnets*, the continental motoring organisations operated a reciprocal arrangement among themselves whereby motorists from half a dozen countries could cross one another's frontiers with a good deal less trouble than the average British tourist was at that time experiencing even in landing at Boulogne. Such benefits were enjoyed by members of the continental associations concerned; why, therefore, should these facilities not be available to the rank and file of British motorists?

To the Touring Club de France, the first to be approached, the suggestion made good sense: it meant more members for them, more tourists for France. They agreed to the A A's proposal, with the proviso that £2,000 be deposited with them by the Association as a guarantee against any member's defaulting or otherwise infringing regulations. The sum was found (characteristically enough, by the bank guarantees of committee members), and the Association turned its attention to the business of cross Channel transport with an eye to the possibility of a more nearly all-embracing *carnet*.

'Now for those wonderful, straight French roads . . .'

Hitherto motor cars crossing the Channel had had to be shipped between Southampton and Le Havre by the old South Western railway company. But now, with a judicious mixture of eloquence and sound business talk, the Association persuaded the South Eastern and Chatham railway (which ran the Dover-Calais and the Folkestone-Boulogne services) to ship motor cars on their regular passenger steamers. This was an incomparable advance on the existing transportation by cargo ship which had involved crating, and was an example of that AA desire for a quick and safe passage which is mirrored today in its advocacy of 'drive on and off' port facilities.

Hence early in 1908 the Association's Secretary was able to report in the press: 'The AA member in search of sunshine finds every difficulty smoothed. . . . He wants to go to Bordeaux and Biarritz, via Boulogne? Very well. Forms, printed in plain, simple language, are ready for him to sign. Deposits are taken at the offices in Coventry Street, tickets issued, seats engaged, petrol commandeered; in fact he and his car are carried about with every possible directness, and without the unpleasant "school treat" feeling engendered by the ordinary touring bureau. He waves his AA permits in the face of humbled frontier officials, and goes on his way rejoicing.'

Members were naturally delighted with this easing of their difficulties. Henceforth the friendly face of an AA representative greeted them on the quayside at Boulogne or Newhaven and their cars were swiftly got on to the road. Further away at Biarritz an agent was stationed for the benefit of members who wished to get their cars from France into Spain.

But the Association's service was not to stop short at the customs shed, despite the solicitude which it showed in (for example) siphoning out members' petrol and storing it for them in those days when one was not allowed to travel with fuel in the tank. Instructions, guides, hints, maps, phrase books, window stickers of continental road signs – any information which might help that new style British traveller, the motorist, in his adventurous penetration of the continent

R

began to pour from Fanum House. An office in Paris became busy with clients. Special patrols – soon to grow into complete staffs, including interpreters – were appointed at the docks. Approved overseas garages and hotels were issued with the familiar Association sign. Agreements were reached with continental authorities regarding licences and registrations. And finally, by a special Order in Council, the AA was authorised by the government to examine and certify on its behalf the fitness of motor cars and drivers for travel abroad.

Motorist (crossing desert). "SO IT WASN'T A MIRAGE AFTER ALL."

The extension of the Association's activities to foreign countries quickly proved to be one of the most important and influential of its many services. In the first place, the service met an existing demand – one which had hitherto been stifled by the difficulties involved in taking a car overseas. In the second, it created a new demand by demonstrating to stay at home members that motoring abroad could now be enjoyed in peace of mind, along with that element of discovery which still gives foreign touring its special excitement and attraction.

Shortly before the first war, the Association set out to identify itself as closely as possible with the Ligue Internationale des Associations Touristes (soon to become the Alliance Internationale de Tourisme), an active organisation born, as early as 1898, out of the various cyclists' touring clubs which had already worked out the basis of a procedure for Britons going abroad. As an international concern, it was felt, the A I T was admirably equipped for extending operations on the continent. And so it proved; for with the first hand experience of the Alliance now supplementing its own intimate knowledge of continental travelling conditions, the A A was able to offer its members unrivalled facilities. Furthermore, as motoring organisations on the A A pattern began to spread throughout the Commonwealth – to South Africa and Canada, to Australia and New Zealand – so the helping hand extended further still. Today some fifty motoring organisations throughout the British Commonwealth, representing about four million motorists, have adopted and adapted the A A badge.

At home, likewise, developments were rapid. Uniformed port officers were appointed in many places where British motorists embarked for destinations overseas, and soon that highly geared mechanism was born which today speeds over 70,000 members on their way abroad in the course of a normal year.

Meanwhile, the hard won influence of the *carnet* steadily increased. It is a matter of history how on one occasion, frustrated in his attempts to ensure motoring facilities in Spain for members, Stenson Cooke set off for Madrid, sought out the national President, offered a substantial guarantee to be lodged in a Madrid bank, and with a few friends started a new motoring club in Spain which could be affiliated to the A I T and bring Spain into its orbit.

Today, as the result of such vigorous pioneering, the ports of Britain and Ireland have become great clearing houses for international motor traffic, as the AA officials who serve them know. As the stream flows through them, amusing memories are left behind. 'We have all had the experience of members who leave documents, passports or money at home,' said one official, 'and even of those who turn up at Folkestone thinking they are at Dover. But we long awaited a member who would arrive with everything in order, except that he had left his car behind. That finally happened recently. A motorist came into the office and pathetically told us that he had parked his car in the town and couldn't for the life of him think where it was. Could *we* trace it? We did!'

Outgoing tourists can be equally forgetful: there was, for instance, the case of the lady who arrived at a port with the conviction that she had left her gas stove burning. A relay of patrols was arranged to rush the key of her house back to London. The end of the story is the obvious one – the stove, of course, was off all the time. Motorists to whom such unusual services are rendered are naturally grateful; but the port staff sometimes feel that gratitude can be over enthusiastically expressed, and one officer still feels a blush coming to his cheeks when he remembers a foreign visitor to whom he had rendered a service showing his indebtedness by flinging both arms round the officer's neck and kissing him soundly on both cheeks.

Headquarters work, too, has its unusual features, especially in the tourist season when substantial staffs in the foreign touring departments are kept busy handling the thousands of queries which pour in every week. But this aspect of the Association's services has been brought to a high peak of efficiency. Twenty-five years ago a reporter from *The Star* noted the time it took for a man behind the counter to produce for him a route from Boulogne to Rome. It took six minutes flat; and with the printed route came excellent road maps of France and Central Europe, neatly tucked up in a special wallet.

The journalist was impressed, as well he might have been. But only the other day I myself made the same experiment. The route – twelve pages of it, accompanied by three booklets of town plans – was handed to me in just two minutes from the word 'go'. And, as I promptly ascertained, I could have had a road route from London to Calcutta without in any way taxing the system.

The secret lies in a plentiful supply of routes – or, rather, of sections of routes – being always on hand, ready printed and ingeniously

PLATE 51

*Britons going abroad (left) –
and visitors
to these islands too (below) –
find the A A port offices
at their disposal.*

*The pattern of the
Automobile Association's
road services
has been followed
in many countries.
Here (right)
the familiar sign
leads the field on
the continent.*

PLATE 52

The seventy or so badges of motoring organisations
which are displayed on these pages
are only some of those which, all across the world,
are linked with the Automobile Association's.
That so many of them display the twin 'A's
is the tribute paid by many daughters to one parent.

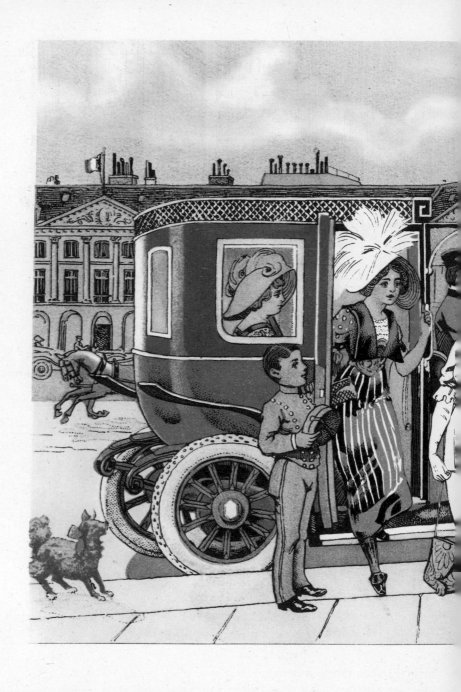

In 1911, when this scene might have taken place in the Place
Vendôme, the AA Paris office had already been established for two years.

"You and your 'All roads lead to Rome'!"

PLATE 54

*The British motorist
may find
unfamiliar signs on the
long straight Autobahn,
the Route Nationale,
or the winding
mountain road which
tempts him overseas.*

filed. Additional information can be quickly typed in, or copies can be
run off on those miniature 'presses' of the foreign routes department,
which also duplicate the descriptive information on the *carnets* themselves. By assembling the printed pages in order, the staff can produce
virtually any standard route that may be called for. Considering that,
in the peak holiday period, requests for foreign routes exceed 2,000
a day, some such streamlined system is obviously essential.

But by no means all requests are for the better known highways.
Some members like to plan, say, an angling holiday, in which they
expect the Association to know – or to find out – the best reaches for
particular kinds of fish, the details of local bait, the angling fees and so
on. Others like to tour places where they can see paintings, or listen
to music, or catch butterflies. None is disappointed.

In this matter of routes, the AA is justifiably proud to have been
the force behind one of the most remarkable highway projects of
modern times – the international road between London and Istanbul.
In 1930 the Association's delegate at the annual general meeting of
the AIT described a dream in which he had envisaged the motoring
and touring organisations of Europe combining in sponsoring such a
highway, via Brussels, Vienna and Belgrade. The project, he suggested, would not only improve communications, and therefore help
motorists, but would also focus political attention on the need to encourage international travel. The idea was taken up with such
enthusiasm that by 1938 – when 1,500 miles were in being – its spon-
sors had a plan to continue the road to Calcutta. And today – when
the AIT represents 110 countries ranging from Iraq to Iceland and
Hungary to Hong Kong – work on a modification avoiding the Iron
Curtain countries is going ahead as part of what is now called the
International Routes Scheme.

Requests for routes to Asia Minor and India are, indeed, commonplace nowadays, and even the overland journey through Africa, from
Algiers down to Cape Town, has passed into the stock of standard
information. Shortly after the war the Association issued a statement

discouraging intending emigrants to South Africa from attempting this particular journey privately by road unless properly equipped, on the grounds that the difficulties were 'almost insuperable' and the risks 'many and real'. Today, however, a twelve page brief is available to interested members, setting out in detail exactly how it can be done. While insisting that the trip across Africa is still an expensive and exacting operation, the AA now declares that – given resourcefulness, careful planning and timing, and a suitably equipped vehicle – it can be accomplished successfully. There follow practical suggestions regarding kit, licences and permits, regulations for crossing the Sahara, and alternative routes – information largely gathered from members who have already made the journey and gratefully reported back their experiences. In six months of a recent year (September to April being the season for such a venture) no fewer than twenty-five AA assisted parties have made the journey. At Fanum House, this request has ceased to be a novelty.

The Association, in fact, has never discouraged the element of adventure in foreign touring. In 1934 it was publicising, in association with the Suomi Touring Club of Finland, a motoring holiday 300 miles beyond the arctic circle. 'Those who undertake the journey,' said a press report at the time, 'will receive a special badge, incorporating a polar bear.' Less tangible incentives included a view of the midnight sun and AA service even in northernmost Lapland. More recently, the foreign routes department has prepared an absorbing summary of an overland journey to the Middle East, India and Australia. Salonika, Istanbul, Damascus, Baghdad, Kandahar, Kabul – the very names along the route, one feels, tracing them on a map with a lingering finger, are milestones to romance.

But can such an astonishing journey still be possible in these days of international tensions and barbed wire frontiers? Apparently it can; for here it is, that fabulous route, confined to a single sheet of foolscap and described in the calm and measured tones of a man who knows his business. Accommodation, he tells us, though 'often of a

simple nature', is available all the way; and 'well sprung vehicles'
will find the going 'very reasonable' through Afghanistan. If this is
not a challenge to adventure, then I have never been a motorist.

Despite such reassurances, however, the thought of a major breakdown in such territory might well deter all but the most stout hearted.
But in western Europe the continental breakdown service, introduced
in 1950, would nowadays cover such an emergency. Its area is divided
into twenty-two zones, each with an accredited A A agent, and each
zone has a code letter marked clearly on the map which the foreign
touring department issues to members motoring abroad. A member
whose private car breaks down beyond local repair can quickly find
the appropriate agent's name and address by means of this code letter,
whereupon the agent takes over, recovers the car, and has it transported to a Channel port. This additional service, incidentally, costs
no extra: it is included in the £3 fee which members pay before
leaving the country.

Less catastrophic breakdowns, which nevertheless cannot be
repaired locally owing to lack of a particular replacement, are likewise tackled with speed and efficiency: a telegram to Fanum House
will in nearly all cases bring the necessary part by air. Within the
past twelve months – to select examples almost at random – a doctor
in Kenya has been sent the spares which he had failed to find anywhere
in the territory, special kinds of weather strip for keeping out sand

have been flown to a member in Aden, and no fewer than eight complete engines have been rushed out in answer to urgent requests.

The longest flight of this kind so far was to Ceylon, where a member had wired the A A in London for new pistons. Another example of the immediate action taken on receipt of such a request is that of the tourist who wired for a certain spare for the hand built car in which he was stranded at Boulogne. The telegram was received only one hour before the works concerned (located well outside London) was due to close for its annual fortnight's holiday. A radio patrol was directed to the factory. He picked up the spare and delivered it to a road patrol who was standing by *en route*. Two and a half hours after the message had been received, the precious part was at Fanum House. Only a little later it was on its way by air across the Channel – just another of the five hundred or so parts which, in one recent year alone, the A A flew out to members in difficulties abroad.

The Association's overseas services quite often find themselves in the public eye, and in December 1951 they contributed a curious footnote to the story of the vanished atom scientist, Professor Pontecorvo. A week before his disappearance the professor had written to the port office at Dunkirk, booking – and paying for – a return passage from Italy by car. His Vanguard was later found abandoned and was recovered by the A A who would, if the car had disappeared with its owner, have been obliged to pay Italian duty on it.

The story belongs to the past: but the A A has plans for the future too, plans involving an increasing use of the air. Only a few years back it realised the inconvenience caused to midland, north country and Scottish members by their having to waste precious time in driving to one of the traditional Channel ports, when a direct air link from, say, Birmingham to the French coast could ferry them and their vehicles abroad in ninety minutes.

The Association, of course, had no desire permanently to enter the business of commercial transport: but it believed that this was one of those matters in which it had to create a precedent. Accordingly it

chartered a Superfreighter and staged just such a flight as it had envisaged. This was such an encouraging success that the A A then felt
that it could retire and leave the field to the commercial operators,
who are in fact adding their own laurel to the Association in its
jubilee year by commencing regular services. When that happens the
Association will be represented at Elmdon, the midland airport, just
as it already is at Ferryfield, Calais and Le Touquet. More and more
members, indeed, are turning to the air as a means of extending their
motoring holiday abroad by those inevitably wasted hours which are
at present taken up in a sea crossing.

Motorists from overseas, whether they belong to affiliated organisations or not, find the A A waiting to welcome them on arrival –
ready to issue them with a temporary driving licence, full information
on touring conditions in Britain, and a copy of *The Highway Code*.
Similarly, in cases when a driving test is required before a licence can
be issued, it is the local office which takes on the responsibility of
examining the foreign visitor and giving him, if necessary, personal
demonstrations of our rules of the road. This is a task which has been
delegated to the A A by the Ministry of Transport – another instance
of the confidence vested in it by public authorities. Such care and shep-
herding becomes increasingly important: motorists from abroad
whose documents were handled by the Association during a recent
year totalled over 26,000, of whom nearly 1,000 were given driving
tests by the Association. Add to those figures the tens of thousands of
British motorists who go abroad under the Association's aegis annually, and the picture is more startling still. It is, indeed, a fair reflec-
tion of the world's largest and most comprehensive motor touring
service that it should handle over 200,000 vehicles entering and
leaving these islands every year and representing a duty liability of
some £20,000,000.

Is it, then, extravagant to claim for the A A that it has shaped the
development of motor touring throughout the world? The facts
speak plainly enough. Many countries (Federal Germany is only the

latest) have modelled their road services on the A A, some of them down to such details as the patrol's polished boots and friendly salute. The Association is constantly invited to demonstrate its methods and equipment overseas. And above all its code of service has taken root wherever its example has been followed.

This, I suggest, is no mean contribution to international good fellowship. And if the A A ever had any qualms at the magnitude of this self appointed task – to include the highways of the whole world in one all-embracing service – these are nowhere discernible in the records. But then, the Association has always taken its own road forward. And it has written its own history on the way.

XIII. OPERATION RESCUE

RAYMOND BAXTER

It could easily have been an operations room at Biggin Hill, aboard HMS Vernon, or at the headquarters of South East Asia Command. There were the same large scale maps, the same patterns of pins and ribbons conveying heaven knew what vital information to the knowledgeable eye, the same atmosphere of easy efficiency and of direct and immediate contact with a world removed from its near-library calm.

The place – in fact, and somewhat to my surprise – really was a nerve centre run on military lines. That the man with the microphone, housed in a glass cubicle, was in touch with nothing more romantic than a yellow and black vehicle proceeding along the Edgware Road only five miles distant in no way detracted from the general effect. That the row of lights before him and the repeating and similar lights on the wall over the telephone desks conveyed nothing more vital to our national security than the availability of the vehicles of the A A emergency service on duty in London that evening did not lessen the impression of orderly urgency and importance.

But then, the operations rooms in London and the provinces *are* important to a very considerable section of the community. For this scene is not confined to the Association's headquarters by Leicester Square, and is to be seen any evening in an ever expanding number of provincial centres. In all of these, men with microphones are in immediate touch with highly trained mobile rescue units moving within a radius of approximately fifteen miles of their control rooms; and the result is that a very large area of the country is covered, day and night, by an umbrella of aid for the motorist in trouble. Soon, I was told, the system will be virtually nationwide.

It seemed to me that the introduction of the A A's radio scheme was a step of outstanding enterprise by an organisation which stood to make no direct financial gain from the expenditure of a considerable amount of capital, and I wondered how it had come about. Radio direction for the taxicab fleet operator is an obvious advantage – the sooner the meter is ticking up with the fare safely in the back seat, the better – but from the A A's point of view it could well be asked 'Why bother?' After all, when the patrolman has been directed to the scene of the breakdown and completed the necessary repair, no charge is made to the member for services rendered. But perhaps the answer can be found in statistics – for although statistics are usually dull and frequently deceptive, they are inseparable from the story of the A A's continuous 'Operation Rescue'. So here is one to begin with.

The breakdown services are used at the rate of around 150,000 times a year.

When I discovered that figure – which has risen steadily, is still rising, and of course does not include the work of the ordinary beat patrol – I was astonished; for despite a consistent mileage of well over 30,000 annually during the last four years I can only recall visual evidence of this A A service on perhaps a half dozen occasions.

Where, then, do all these Sir Galahad acts occur? Well, bearing in

mind the tens of thousands of miles of road in Great Britain upon which the Association maintains its paternal watch over 5,282,222 vehicles, one must concede the possibility that much rescue work may pass unnoticed by any individual. (This figure, of course, includes *all* types of vehicle, whatever their ownership. But then, so does the paternal watch of the Association. For example, as a gesture to chivalry the breakdown crews are instructed to assist an unaccompanied lady driver in distress whether she is a member or not.) And it is easier to maintain that watch with the aid of radio.

It can scarcely be denied that the tremendous demand for roadside aid reflects upon the reliability of the motor car as a conveyance. At first sight, the coldly written figure of 150,000 breakdowns per year dealt with by this service alone may give one pause to consider the possibility that the horseless carriage is still in its experimental stage. But, as a patrolman said to me one morning as we took 'char' together at one of those converted double decker bus buffets which occasionally appear at thirsty moments along our trunk roads, 'The modern car is a little more reliable than its owner allows it to be'.

The man was right, of course. The majority of rescue operations undertaken by the Association are occasioned by electrical and fuel feed failures, and this must inevitably reflect unfavourably on the

care and attention which the average owner driver is prepared to devote to his car. Laziness is the main culprit: so long as the 'old bus' behaves herself we are liable to leave her largely to her own devices. Again, servicing costs money – a lot of money today – and money spent in maintaining an already expensive article is, paradoxically, begrudged by most people.

So there are roadside breakdowns too serious to be dealt with by the patrol on his motor cycle outfit or else occurring at times when he is not on the road; and again the detailed statistics of the Association's records are relevant, and ironically amusing. For they illustrate a classic example of 'the cussedness of nature'.

Nothing could be more depressing than a breakdown at night in the pouring rain. Yet those are precisely the conditions under which half of them occur. Of the total of some 6,000 rescue operations conducted in the London area during a typical month, over 4,000 are at night and two-thirds of these during bad weather. It was to ease the lot of the unhappy motorist caught under these depressing circumstances that the AA's night emergency service was instituted.

In speaking of it, one of the officials who played a prominent part in its creation said 'Of course, all the night service chaps have the AA outlook on life. They don't expect to work normal hours. They regard any breakdown as a personal challenge to their skill and initiative. They are enthusiasts'. And this was no boast. It was an accurate assessment of the men who operate the service.

But let us consider what is meant by this service in both its day and night phases. Printed in every handbook are the following words: 'The free breakdown service is complementary to the AA road service. It enables members whose vehicles have broken down on the road to obtain free assistance from a garage if an AA patrol is not readily available'.

In other words, if you're stuck, the Association's object is to help you to get unstuck as cheaply and efficiently as possible. By day it may do so through its patrols or by directing you to a nearby garage, but at night most garages are shut and public transport is scarce or non-existent. The A A has been conscious of this – and has experimented with night patrols – since 1924, but only in these radio days can there be effective coverage. And in fact, with the introduction of radio after the war, the number of cases in which aid was given jumped immediately by nearly fifty per cent.

Hence, within the areas of radio control, Land Rovers cruise from 6 pm to 9 am and at other times when help may be hard to obtain. Normally crewed by one man each, their equipment is the result of years of experience. They can tow almost any car, for instance, and they can draw a trailer into which a motor cycle can readily be loaded if necessary. High lift jacks are carried, not only to facilitate wheel changing but to provide the equivalent of a portable inspection hoist. Then there is a slave battery, which solves seventy-five per cent of starting problems on stranded vehicles. The equipment carried is not limited by the capacity of the sidecar of the ordinary patrol; and the weather protection afforded by the enclosed cab of the vehicle, with its comfortable seats and heater, can mean longer hours on the night roads in winter without loss of human efficiency.

But night assistance is not limited to the A A's own vehicles. In this, as in all technical matters, the Association works in the closest co-operation with the garage men. In London seven twenty-four hour garages are actually connected to the radio net, in direct and constant communication with Fanum House. Thus – should there be no Land Rover available for a given rescue at any time, or should one of the radio garages be nearer the spot – the man on duty would call out the garage crew, in exactly the same way as he would summon his own vehicle, to assist the stranded driver. In addition, of course, the 109 garages operating a twenty-four hour service in the London area may be summoned by telephone under similar circumstances. And the bill for all emergency repairs on the road, not involving new parts, is footed by the Automobile Association.

These 'radio garages' lie generally along the perimeter of Greater

London, and the policy is for the Land Rovers to work from the centre outwards to this perimeter and for the garage vehicles to range further afield. But all are the responsibility of the night service manager, under whom a staff at Fanum House works in two shifts through the dark hours.

At Bank Holidays and at weekends (and the service may be called on well over 1,000 times in a single weekend) the difficulties confronting the motorist in trouble are comparable to those which beset him at night. Overtime rates may make it difficult for the small garage or service station proprietor in a thinly populated area to remain open as long as he wishes, and despite the millions of pleasure bound motorists on the roads at such times the facilities available to the family man defeated by an ignition fault while the baby yells for his tea can be so inadequate as to constitute a major domestic crisis. Therefore the Land Rovers back up the work of the patrolmen on road service outfits who are also on duty at holiday periods, and a telephone call to the Automobile Association will bring an immediate and practical response.

As the man on duty by day or night takes particulars of each call for aid, a glance at the lights (showing green for 'available', red for 'engaged', or white for 'off duty') will advise him of the readiness with which assistance can be brought to bear. As work is assigned, the touch of a key brings the repeating lights over the telephone tables into line. By the time the controller is handing on particulars of the intended rescue, via the radio microphone, to the crew nearest the job, the member will have been informed whether to look out for A A or garage aid and how soon this assistance will reach him.

But how about the receiving end of this radio control? When I went out with a London based vehicle (by night, for the romance of it) I thought that I would be in for an easy and probably amusing evening. It was amusing, for in such company it could not possibly have been dull. But easy! Even as a spectator I found it exhausting. At 6 pm, at their depot in the Fulham Palace Road, the men of the

PLATE 55

*A radio call is put through
from the scene of a breakdown;
within minutes
a tow is arranged,
and a car is hauled
to a garage.
Hundreds of times daily
such rescue work
is carried out
through the A A's use
of radio links.*

night service parade for duty in the slightly military atmosphere which one notes frequently on the operational side of the Association's work. And after a check by the inspector, away go the vehicles to take up stations in their areas.

But even before these target destinations are reached the chances are that at least two of the vehicles will be diverted to jobs. I travelled with an ex-squadron leader, and as the loudspeaker in the Land Rover's cab cut into our conversation I was impressed by the clarity of the signal and the excellence of the RT procedure. Again I was reminded of my thoughts of Biggin Hill.

The job of a night service inspector is self explanatory, and I rode with him to see as much as possible in a given time. In fact, we reached our first job before the patrol who had been detailed to it. A member had a puncture and had called assistance for the wheel change. There were no complications. The job took four minutes; but, as the inspector said, as he cleaned his hands with the soft soap and towel carried for the purpose, 'Why should *he* get dirty? Maybe he's going out to dinner'.

At this time, one vehicle was on its way to an electrical fault in Whitechapel, another was engaged upon a case of fuel starvation in Hampstead, and a third was hurrying to a worried chauffeur in Maida Vale. As we moved off, a lady stopped her car in front of us and asked for a certain garage. She was not a member and said so. When the inspector lifted his handset and called Fanum House to check the location of the garage 'before her very eyes' she was flabbergasted. We guided her there in a matter of minutes and she joined the Association on the spot.

So it went on, hour after hour through the night, with vehicles moving almost without respite from job to job. Not until after 1 am was there much of a lull, with time for sandwiches and a thermos of something warming before the commercial traffic came rolling in towards the markets. And then, when it comes to a wheel change on a fifteen ton diesel, the member does not call for assistance just to keep

T

'I think it's only fair to tell you I'm not a member.'

his hands clean. These 'lorry jobs', like the vehicles themselves, are man sized affairs – and the more welcome, therefore, to the 'enthusiasts' who answer the calls.

During the course of the evening the technical problems faced by the rescuers were varied in the extreme. No two jobs were identical: and therein lies much of their appeal to the men whose job it is to 'cope'. There was, for instance, the worried lady who had found herself descending the slope of Trafalgar Square with no brakes at all. Fortunately the traffic lights were with her, and we found her in Northumberland Avenue shaken but intact. Topping up the master cylinder of the hydraulic system restored her brakes and nerves, and enabled her to continue to her home in Battersea in safety.

At a little after midnight petrol was supplied to a stranded musician homeward bound from a professional engagement, who was unlucky enough to 'conk out' immediately in front of Buckingham Palace at the beginning of the Royal Mile. The Land Rover's arrival coincided with that of a police car, for roadside parking is liable to attract immediate official reaction in that corner of London. Shortly after this the inspector was directed to investigate the case of a vehicle, apparently abandoned, parked almost in the centre of a side street not far from Soho Square. It had been spotted by one of the drivers *en route* to a job. He had reported to 'Fanum One', the control, who had in turn called 'Yellow King', ourselves. The car bore no AA badge, there were no signs of the driver in the immediate vicinity, and hence the matter was passed over to the police with our inspector standing by until they arrived.

A minor snag with a pre-selector gearbox was cured in minutes, much to the surprise of the clergyman at the wheel. Faulty light bulbs were replaced, a fuel pump filter cleaned, and a crumpled wing eased from a wheel with which it was in immediate contact following a brush with a lamp post. Only once that night, in fact, were the crews beaten. A broken halfshaft necessitated an immediate call to the nearest all-night garage, which had a breakdown crane on the spot for the tow within ten minutes.

But whether the job was large or small, simple and swift or long and complex, the fundamental approach of the night staff seemed to me to be one of genuine eagerness to 'get cracking'. For they are happy men. They have their grouses, of course. They get fed up like the rest of us. They have their own ideas on how things should be done, and on what is a waste of time and money. But they seldom seek another job. They like the one they do – and, because they like it, they do it well.

As I turned my own car for home after my night on the road with them, I was myself a happy man. I had been infected by the spirit that radiates from their sturdy yellow vehicles, a spirit that is all too often forgotten in these troubled, indifferent days. It was the feeling of pride in a job well done.

'That's nothing – you should see my kitchen!'

XIV. LONDON PILOT

KAY FULLER

As the motoring tourist crosses the invisible boundaries of London it is borne in upon him that his difficulties are increasing. Perhaps he has made his way up from Dover or Southampton and already spent several hours in a car with a lefthand drive wondering why the mad English must travel on the wrong side of the road. But so far he has remained cheerful. He is, no doubt, on vacation, and there are pleasing prospects ahead. He shrugs his shoulders at English nonconformity, and presses on.

Now London begins to overtake him. There is a marked increase of vehicles before and behind, giant red buses are hemming him in, and zebra crossings hold him up every few yards. Nor is this all: soon he will find himself offered a bewildering choice of direction. Vast junctions appear, it seems to him without warning. Borne away upon the fast moving stream, he finds too late that his involuntary selection has led him several miles along the wrong road. He ventures a short cut back again. An alarming amount of time passes and doubt begins to creep in. His family and friends in the back seat peer anxiously out of the windows, offering unhelpful advice. All the streets look alike. The houses are grains of sand in a desert. Is this the fatal crossroads, or some other, or what? Where, in heaven's name, are they?

They are lost; but they are still in London. It may be wondered whether anyone really knows the size of the place or how many people live in it, for of course it all depends what one means by 'London'. But if one combines the County of London and the City of London one has an agglomeration with a population larger than that of Norway and an area of 117 square miles. As for its traffic, the statistics are

astronomical. Was our tourist intimidated by those red buses wedged
beside him? No wonder. They carry more than 3,000,000,000 passengers a year, which means there are quite a few of them on the roads.
Every day 8,000 of them round Hyde Park Corner. But that is a
mere nothing to the total number of vehicles which daily pass this
point: it is nearer 80,000. It will be understood, then, that to enter
this vortex driving a strange car, or without a good knowledge of
London routes and traffic regulations, is to enter upon a period of difficulty and anxiety liable to end in nervous exhaustion if not collapse.

This was realised some years ago by the AA, whose first step was
to arrange for experienced independent drivers to meet members from
overseas or the provinces, to take over the controls, and to drive
through the congestion of the metropolitan area, handing over again
to the owner when the open road was reached. This was an excellent
arrangement and proved so popular that the demand grew steadily.

It was then that a senior official of the AA proposed a revolutionary
idea. This was that the Association should have its own pilots and
that they should be women drivers. The first part of his proposition
was considered reasonable; the second downright shocking. Women
drivers had acquired and kept a number of unpleasant names. The
senior official was, however, a persistent and ultimately convincing
advocate. He had spent many years with REME during the second
world war. He had seen how the drivers of the women's services had
handled every kind of vehicle from a heavy lorry to a jeep. There, he
said, was a reservoir of really first class material to be tapped. And so
in 1950 the first two London pilots were appointed to the AA staff.
One had been a driving instructor with the ATS, the other a driver
with the WAAF. They were provided with a smart and distinctive
uniform (which soon earned them, around Fanum House, the name of
the 'Khaki Kuties') and they set to work.

Today there are six of these pilots, and an average of 5,000 motorists make use of their services each year. For a small fee, and by
writing to the Association twenty-four hours in advance, a member

can be met on the outskirts and piloted skilfully into or across London
in the least possible time. Or he can ask for his new car to be collected
from a saleroom and driven to Tilbury for shipment overseas. One
film star even cabled from Hollywood 'Please run in my new car, then
deliver it to the airport to meet me', and had to worry no more.

More difficult was to tow a racehorse which started to stampede in
its trailer, but the six pilots have many stories to tell of unexpected
situations and difficulties overcome. One overseas visitor, for instance,
bought a British car and proceeded to take it on the road. Then it
occurred to him, reasonably enough, that it would be pleasant to drive
through Hyde Park. But could he get into the park? By no means.
Confused by unfamiliar gears, bewildered by the traffic lanes, he drove
round and round the Marble Arch until he was dizzy. At last he man-
aged to drop anchor at a telephone and rang the AA. A London pilot
came to his rescue, took him into the park, and there gave him a driving lesson until his nerve was restored.

The pilots are prepared for most things, but they occasionally get a
shock. A member in Chester filled in the printed application form,
giving his make of car and registration number and asking for a pilot
to meet him at Hendon. Armed with these details, she stationed herself at the rendezvous, ready for the job and wearing her usual expression of cheerful welcome. Suddenly, as a vehicle drew alongside
bearing the number she sought, her expression changed to something
more suitable. Inside there were men in top hats, layers of flowers –
and a coffin. It was then that she realised she was to have the somewhat dispiriting responsibility of piloting a hearse to a cemetery.

But there are plenty of less solemn engagements, and some that
show the particular usefulness of women as pilots. There was the occasion, for instance, when a young married couple had to attend a
reception and could not leave their brand new baby behind. So a London pilot drove them to the reception, kept the baby fed, dry and
happy for several hours in the car, and then drove the family home
again. On another occasion a pilot had to drive with a goat nibbling at

PLATE 57 *Strangers to the capital,*
they find traffic conditions perplexing in a huge misty city.
But the smiling, confident London pilot will be there to guide them through.

PLATE 58

Khaki-uniformed girls like these
are conversant
with that tortuous maze
of streets, squares,
roundabouts and alleys
which is London.

her neck: but – as an animal lover – she quite enjoyed the experience.

There is indeed, as the senior London pilot says, more in the job than meets the eye. The pilots need to have a good deal of resource, to dispense all kinds of information to the enquiring visitor beside them and, above all, to be able to handle without hesitation any make of car, old or new, British or foreign. One pilot was asked how many different makes of cars she had driven. A vast rally took shape in her mind: the elderly couple from Cumberland with their equally elderly limousine, the Americans with the big hydromatic, the Indians and Italians and South Africans with righthand drive, lefthand drive, preselector gears, gear levers on the wheel, gear levers on the floor, gadgets and lack of gadgets. Well, how many different makes *had* she in fact driven?

Perhaps, she concluded, it would be simpler to say how many she had *not* driven.

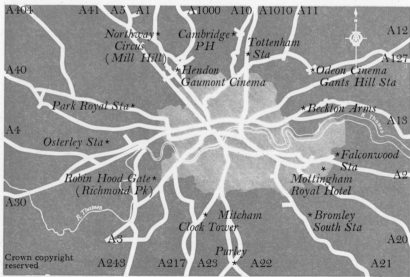

These are the principal meeting points and throughroutes used by the London pilots.

U

XV. EMERGENCY CALL

BRYAN MORGAN

It is strictly forbidden for an A A patrolman to touch liquor whilst he is in uniform: but there is nothing at all to stop him enjoying a quiet pint when he is off duty, especially when he is with his fiancée. And that is just what Patrol No 9089 was on his way to do at about eight in the evening on Friday, 15th August 1952.

It was raining on the way to the Exmoor Forest Hotel at Simons-bath – raining very heavily, even by local standards. But a decidedly wet patrolman arrived at the inn, only to be met with the news that a resident was having a little ignition trouble. Although off duty, he of course crossed the yard to rectify the fault. It took only ten minutes, after which he was asked to help the landlord in clearing some drains. That done, the patrol was free to return to his well earned pleasures. In fact, he had his hand on the back door, when the thing happened. . . .

The Forest Hotel stands by a trout stream, and that was swollen enough. But suddenly the patrol saw water appearing from a new direction, down the opposite side of the combe: and this was no stream but a ten foot high wall of destruction. He got indoors and closed the door behind him. A few seconds later the water opened it again. And in came Niagara.

Within minutes the rear rooms were flooded to the ceilings: the front rooms, on a higher level, were six feet deep in water. From the packed bar the patrol escorted guests upstairs to safety. Then he and the landlord surveyed the situation. The great wave had passed by now, but the whole lower part of the inn was filled like a tank with water which could not escape. The job, therefore, was to break open the doors and windows, and this job was done. It sounds simple, but

it involved five hours of wading and submarine swimming, in darkness and amid water on which floated such surrealistic debris as bee-
hives, tables and ninepins.

When all that could be done had been done it was three in the
morning. For the rescuers there was time for an hour or two of sleep
before daylight and the task of getting guests' cars on the road again.
And that sleep was undoubtedly deepened by the patrol's presence of
mind in seizing a bottle of rum as he swam through the bar.

Although nobody realised it at the time, such was the start of a
disaster which was to take some thirty lives – a cruel disaster for
peacetime, but one which was not without lesser precedents for the
A A. All across the granite breadth of Exmoor phenomenal rain –
over nine inches of it before the night was through – had piled up
behind temporary dams and then broken through them with renewed
force. But on that Friday night the situation was felt only as a number
of scattered incidents. By the sea at Lynton, for instance, Patrol No
4628 was roused in the small hours by refugees escaping from the
flooded twin village of Lynmouth below. Again, just what had happened was then in doubt, for communications were broken: but again
there was work to be done by a disciplined man. And all through the
long, lightning torn night that patrol too was engaged in operations
of rescue and succour.

Daybreak saw the end of the torrential rains and the beginning of
an ironic hot spell which was to last throughout the Lynmouth rescue operations and develop an almost unendurable stench from
smashed sewers, spilt petrol and decay. It saw, too, the first chance to
appreciate just what had happened. One branch of the Lyn river, falling 1,500 feet, had changed its course: and now, three times its normal width, it ran down the High Street between shattered shop fronts.
Vehicles, thirty-ton boulders, tree trunks which had been awaiting
the saw mills, the carcases of drowned cattle, and what one observer
described as 'thousands of tons of God knows what' had been flung
across the streets. Miles out to sea the Bristol Channel ran brown

with flotsam, debris and mud as it bore away many thousands of
millions of gallons of flood water. Few air raids ever produced a more
terrible dawn.

An hour or two later an inspector arrived, having grasped the
situation from a brief report on the 7 am BBC news and having immediately set out over flooded roads and uncertain bridges. He saw at
once that this was no isolated incident – not one of the thousand and
one minor crises with which, however unexpectedly they may arise,
an officer can deal on his own considerable initiative. It was a civil
emergency, such as may make any AA man a member of an im-
promptu working party; and this AA man applied to it a drill tested
in such cases. He thought first of human lives, secondly of diverting
traffic from the area, and thirdly of the eventual need to rescue trapped
or damaged cars.

Since the danger to life was now over, the inspector rallied as many
men as he could and with them surveyed the whole Exmoor area,
where rivers changed their courses every few hours and thirty bridges
were down. Whilst this work was being carried out, the Lynton
patrolman was left in charge of operations in the devastated village to
such an extent that his house was turned into a one man enquiry office
for lost cars. And it was several hours more before the Association
had sufficient information to put out a concerted effort on Exmoor.

But it was concentrated enough then, despite the fact that other
parts of the west, such as Plymouth and Sherborne, also called for urgent attention. From depots at Broad Clyst and South Molton, at
Bridgwater and Barnstaple, signs were rushed: from Bristol and Exeter and Bournemouth and Cardiff patrolmen moved in: from London
the Association's road manager came to direct operations. At the
peak there were fifty AA men – in many cases supported by their
wives and families – working like five hundred in the Lynmouth area.

On the approach roads 200 more signs, six control points, and later
an AA mobile office, were set up to divert the motorists and coach
parties who were expecting to find Lynmouth still the picture post-

card village of honeymoon hotels and cream teas which it had been once upon a time. Equipped with special telephone lines only twenty-four hours after the first flooding, the office often provided the only means of local communications and was organised as efficiently as a battle headquarters. Time and again on the moor, where ponies stampeding amongst packed relief convoys added to the chaos, patrols found vehicles bogged down or stranded by eighteen-foot gaps cut through roads by new watercourses – and got them to safety, even if it implied manhandling cars hundreds of feet up through thick woods or edging back those which were hanging perilously over gorges.

Messages had to be passed from anxious friends: one patrolman, for instance, spent a whole day in scrambling across streams and up one-in-four hills to despatch telegrams. Another had to drag from the floods a caravan from which two holiday makers had escaped just before it was carried a mile downstream. And a third drove all over the moor to find a Surrey licensee, in response to a call from a relative for whom other means of contact had failed. But for all that the greatest work was done in the ghost town of Lynmouth itself.

There there were quickly specialists enough to deal with human needs – the police, the Salvation Army, the WVS, the fire and ambulance brigades – while later civil and army engineers began the task of blasting away 200,000 tons of boulders and bulldozing roads. The AA men worked in enthusiastically with all of these, and in at least one case a patrol who had spent a week in continuous work under the Association and had then been told to take a rest was found just as hard at work on the eighth day, having exchanged his khaki for the black of the St John Ambulance. But the AA staff now knew that it could revert to a job with which it was charged by the authorities and for which it was well equipped – the rescue and identification of vehicles. For both of these activities the headquarters were to be a new mobile office in Lynton.

In one place, for example, there were fifty vehicles which would be isolated when a necessary and deliberate change in the course of the river took place, and it was under the direction of the AA men that these were safely hauled out of several feet of sludge in the few hours available, the last car being rescued one minute before the deadline. One sapper certainly showed such ability in this delicate work that a patrolman shouted to him 'You ought to be working for us', but *he* could give the reply 'Ought to be? I am, when I'm not on flipping national service'.

In another spot, it was on the initiative of the Association that a road was forced across two rivers and amid boulders to rescue a private hire coach on which a local owner's livelihood depended. Elsewhere a bus was rescued from deep sand, and a car was found which could only be salvaged by being elevated bodily on a mechanical shovel. And, finally, it was a senior AA executive – one who had tramped many tough miles in gum boots – who, when the central problem of getting the cars stranded in Lynmouth up to the safety of Lynton presented itself, came out with one of those bright ideas which star the history of the Association.

'Use the cliff railway,' he suggested. And that was how it was done.

By such means nearly 100 towable vehicles were saved from further damage, though many had been deep in water. One, for instance, harboured a two-pound trout, and several more needed hours of flushing out before they could be driven away. But every battle claims its dead, and there were as many cars damaged beyond repair. Two were supporting a wrecked house: another had been so assaulted by boulders that it was squashed into the semblance of a single plate of steel: and the sea had taken sixty or more, some of which could only be located by frogmen. The patrols, who in their time had played many parts, had now to turn themselves into beachcombers and mudlarks, working against time and tide. At every low water twenty or so were scouring the shore or knee deep in the sea, looking for a number plate, ignition key, membership badge or any identifiable component which would give the owner of an overturned vehicle news of the loss of his property and evidence for a future insurance claim.

There was a week or more of such work, often until late at night and by floodlight; but at the end of this the crisis was over. Enquiries were still coming in to the mobile offices and would continue to do so for weeks more: convoys bringing relief had to be routed: further cars remained to be 'located' before the list totalled 250 or so: and some vehicles had to remain safe but stranded until new Bailey bridges followed the one which was opened on Saturday, 23rd August. But the first unbelievable chaos had been cleared: and when the A A's employees raised over £550 for the relief fund they were thinking not merely of the losses of Lynmouth itself but of the untiring work of fifty of their colleagues in aiding that clearance.

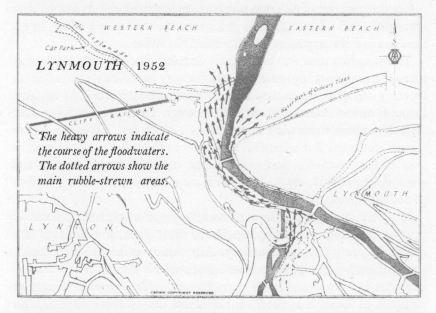

Lynmouth was the most spectacular of the national disasters in which Association men – aided by a tradition of military discipline and fine communications – have preserved lives and cars. But it was

far from being the only one. In the winter of 1939, when there were
very few able-bodied men to spare, the Association somehow rushed
forty of them up to Lincolnshire to divert traffic from waterlogged
areas, and a similar service was performed in the west country and
Yorkshire seven years later. Not all such operations turned on the
weather: there was the Harrow rail smash of October 1952, for instance, when ambulance ferry work and the swift skill with oxy-
acetylene cutters of A A technicians saved many from pain or death.
There was a fire on Jersey a little later, when off-duty patrolmen
worked through the small hours. And in civil emergencies at many
other times the nation has been grateful for some such concerted
operation by the A A.

But the greatest of all takes one back to angry elements, and to that
spring of 1953 when 100 mph gales met high tides and when, in its
first week, February most terribly filled the dykes.

The situation then was less clearly dramatic than at Lynmouth, and
more of a continual nightmare in which every patrolman was called on
to carry out policing duties. For all down the east coast of Britain,
through seven counties from Scarborough to Deal, hundreds lost
their lives and thousands their homes as the sea lashed in across
coastal defences. But a handful of instances from the logs of the four
area offices involved, during the night of 1st February and in the
week that followed, can provide at least a series of lightning flashes
out of that storm rent sky.

In Nottingham, then, the area secretary was awakened at 4 am by
the police calling on his organisation to erect signs, and had over 100
set up before noon the next day. After these came hundreds more
signs, directing the 2,500 rescue lorries which thronged the narrow
East Anglian roads and keeping traffic away from routes in danger of
collapse. In the days of bitter snow which followed there were men on
duty at an improvised headquarters in Louth, and at a mobile office in
the evacuated area of Mablethorpe and Sutton where the floods had
rivalled Lynmouth's.

PLATE 59

*When disaster
struck a seaside village
at Lynmouth (above),
and an express train
at Harrow (left),
the A A
had its part to play.*

PLATE 60

*These pictures
tell their own story of
the Association's work
during the east coast
floods of 1953.*

In Fenland fresh water had wreaked almost as much havoc as had salt water elsewhere, and the Association's Norwich office became a central pool of information for the police and the post office, the railways and the bus companies. At King's Lynn there was a mobile office, and at Harwich eight A A men controlled all the town's traffic for five days and nights.

It was Chelmsford's area, however, which had the greatest task to do: for it included not only tragic Canvey Island (where the Land Rover at work was directed by the A A's first long distance use of radio communications) but such places as Brightlingsea, St Osyth, Wallasea and Jaywick – in which latter a patrolman's enterprise in saving pets and livestock earned him a decoration. All over this area the A A men worked like demons, and often for a fortnight without rest. They found a route to the Tilbury ferry; they cleared a road of boats at Manningtree; they worked at upper windows to get residents out, or tea in, at Brightlingsea; and elsewhere they spent days up to their waists in water, using boats as battering rams as they rescued not merely people and vehicles but rescue trucks themselves.

Across the Thames in Maidstone's area there was work to be done, too. Men were drawn in to the damaged region: a hand was lent in the building of pontoons: and when DUKWs out rescuing sheep became fouled by bushes now subaqueous, a patrol who knew every inch of the road had to turn river pilot and navigate them to safety.

Even when the worst was over there was – once again, but this time over hundreds of square miles – the patient work of salvage, as vehicles were hauled out of slime or dug from six-foot deep deposits of sand. Everywhere in the area the A A suddenly found itself, after its experience at Lynmouth, regarded as a national expert on reconditioning techniques. And that trust was justified, for the Association's men damaged not a single vehicle.

The part played in the east coast floods by the staff of the Association is all the more remarkable since other members of it were simultaneously dealing with a disaster brought about by the same hurricanes

up in north Aberdeenshire. There, hundreds of trees lay across roads
snarled up with telephone wires. One patrolman, having rescued a
woman from a cottage menaced by falling branches, found his route
cut off on both sides and had to leave along a railway line. When
another tree fell in his face blocking *that*, he knew that he had one more
job to do – and ran to alert the nearest signal box.

Hence, through the activities of its local servants – some of whom
themselves suffered loss of property and others of whom made private
offers of food and beds to the homeless – many lives and much property were saved by the A A. But for all that the tributes and letters of
appreciation which flowed in afterwards from individuals and institutions were a treasured surprise to the men involved. There had been
peril on the land, and they had done their duties as part of a great
organisation. It seemed as simple as that.

XVI. ALL THE YEAR ROUND

BRYAN MORGAN

The AA's year – not surprisingly – begins on 1st January. In fact, even as the bells are pealing out across an icy Britain, the night emergency services are maintaining their vigilance: men in lighted offices are answering telephone calls, including some from revellers who have lost the way home, and men in vehicles are even a little more busily engaged than usual. For at this festive season such activities as fishing in drains for lost ignition keys or picking up forgotten theatre tickets have supplemented more normal activities.

Nine hours later the routine work of the year begins, at least in those uncivilised parts of Britain where men cannot recover at leisure from Hogmanay. The work is routine, that is, in so far as any activity can be called routine in an organisation whose rhythm is the rhythm of the year itself. For though there are certain departments of the AA whose pace varies little with the months, and others which follow patterns dictated by the sittings of Parliament or the sequence of quarter days and auditors' visits, to a surprising degree the diverse departments of the Association are influenced by the changes in the year. It is hence not inappropriate to cast a final backward glance over the AA in this calendar form.

Before the crocuses are in bloom, then, and whilst much of the work of the home touring department concerns such mundane matters as routing double decker buses, foreign touring finds holiday queries beginning in order that shipping space may be reserved in advance. Only a little later the technical department registers a peak in the inspection of secondhand cars, and the legal experts find an increase in the number of cases involving hire purchase agreements. For in this

daffodil time a young man's fancy may turn to thoughts of more
prosaic things than love.

The patrolman's thoughts around this season, however, are likely
to be less cheerful. Even if February and March bring no national
weather emergencies, he may have on his own initiative to give a
fireman's lift for a mile to a lady member whose car is snowed up, and
then work all through the night to rescue the car itself from five foot
drifts. He may have to help the police in dragging an icy river for a
suicide's body, or labour up a fell to take hot food to a snowbound
invalid, or rescue a trapped mountain climber. And behind all this
there is the routine work, and the trivial incidents too. Advising a
travelling circus where it can buy meat enough for eight lions, sewing
up with a boot lace the broken driving belt of a veteran car, getting a
baby to sleep by rocking a car, or recovering some children's books
lost on Dartmoor – all such things have to be attended to, in addition
to more normal services, whatever the weather and however blue the
greatcoated patrol's fingers may be. So too – as all the year round –
anybody now tuning in on a frequency of about 85 megacycles would
be struck by a ceaseless interchange of information between radio
patrol or Land Rover and control, as the watch on the roads goes on.

Soon one of the milestones in the A A year is passed with the distribution of a new edition of the annual handbook. This is no mere
matter of pushing a few envelopes into pillar boxes but is, on the contrary, a major logistic operation. With over 1,500,000 copies to be
distributed (weighing about 500 tons and with pages which would, if
spread out, cover an area of five square miles), the very job of
addressing is a considerable engineering feat, involving the shifting
of twenty tons of embossed plates and keeping several high speed
machines busy for a full month.

After such ponderous considerations it is pleasant to move forward
into fresher air, and towards the prospect of flowers on the tables of
the A A's reception halls and white covers on the patrolmen's caps.
But on that journey into sunlight there is an unnerving moment to be

passed early in April; and it is certain that if any of the imposts now laid on hard pressed motorists is not removed in a Budget it is not through lack of spirited agitation on the part of the A A. But the first sting of even an unpopular Budget is forgotten when, in mid-April, the weather map is put aside with hopes that no freak snowfalls will cause it to be set up again for many months.

If it is not, the information bureau men can devote all their attention to those touring enquiries which arrive in bewildering variety as the year gathers pace from Easter onwards. 'Can you give me a route for a trip on horseback from Land's End to John o' Groats?', 'Should I – an American – wear a kilt at highland games?', 'Where are the best mud baths in Germany?' – the answers to all these are necessary to ensure *somebody's* happy holiday: and as a speciality of these scented evenings there are also quite a few snap queries around 8 pm for short after-dinner drives. The information staff are ready to state where glow worms can be found or the whereabouts of the most interesting rock pools on the south coast, and are even prepared for the member who asks for a route to show where he has been rather than where he is going. But they hope that the querying season will not produce a poser quite as extraordinary as one which came their way a summer or two back.

'Where,' two naval men asked, 'can we find a line of trees on the French Riviera with their trunks exactly twelve feet apart.' For the benefit of those who would like to play their own 'Twenty Questions' on this one, the reason for the enquiry is printed upside down at the bottom of the page.

But now, with more motorists on the road, there are more unlucky motorists, and the legal department is hence at its busiest. The peak is not a sharp one, for fog and ice can cause accidents just as congested streets can and the work of supplying legal defence and advice, of

They wanted to sling hammocks.

SPRING

*Cap (or helmet),
tunic, breeches,
leggings, boots
and gloves.*

SUMMER

*White
cap-cover;
no gloves.*

recovering money in and out of court, must go on all through the year. At any time a railway engine may set fire to a car, or an insurance company misunderstand the word 'corgi' and issue a puzzled owner of a motor scooter with a canine insurance policy. At all times there continues that basic work of untangling the complexities of

AUTUMN
*Waterproof
cap-cover,
coat and leggings;
gloves.*

WINTER
*Short
overcoat
and gloves.*

third party claims and owner-driver insurance, of contesting technical-
ities before magistrates' benches and taking important matters of
principle to the courts of appeal, of fighting on a member's behalf for
£5 or £5,000. But in high summer the routine troubles *do* increase
in number, whilst in addition disputes with hotels and questions aris-

ing from the things which seem to go wrong with cars only when they cross the English Channel keep the learned advisers of the Association working late into the luminous evenings.

Throughout high summer the AA takes even more fully to the road, in tune with those members whose demand for home touring routes steadily accelerates to a midsummer peak and whose enquiries on accommodation now exceed 5,000 each month. The area road managers, who may have risked chilblains through the winter in investigating ice covered junctions and surfaces cracked with frost, now find the balance of their attention swinging towards hotel matters. With June busting out all over (and not least in the little gardens round the telephone boxes), the patrolman's life seems an attractive one – and in fact applications to join the patrol staff show a sharp rise in the spring and summer, though the Association itself wisely prefers not to take on a man until he has served a probationary period under harsher conditions. The mobile offices are out on circuit now, bringing AA facilities to such temporarily busy corners of Britain as holiday camps, art festivals and agricultural shows: the Land Rovers are there serving areas of Scotland and Ireland so lonely that in one of them the local patrol has been summoned in an emergency by the firing of a shotgun across a lake: the port officers may be working eighteen hours on end and handling nearly two thousand vehicles a day: the continental breakdown service has most calls upon it: and the London pilot and driver services are in great demand by visitors from many nations. So the AA year approaches its turning point in late July, when the membership department is able to report its own peak in enrolment.

August Bank Holiday brings a break to some – but not to the patrols, for this is a time when long hours must be worked by the men of what has been called the world's largest private army. Those hours will certainly involve such normal services to members as writing out emergency routes. But they might also involve tasks as varied as putting out a fire in a hayfield, discreetly returning the top of a swim suit

PLATE 61

All the year round
sudden emergencies
may call on the resources
of the Automobile Association.

PLATE 62

All the year round, too –
though sometimes enlivened
by the unexpected incident – there continues
a routine programme of service
to the travelling public.

TULIP
FIELDS

CENSUS
POINT

to a lady who has been embarrassingly divorced from it, digging a
member's dog out of a rabbit hole, helping a radio commentator to
rectify a fault in his microphone, chasing a car which has left a garage
with no oil in its gearbox, adapting a spare sparking plug from a
combine harvester to fit an American car, repairing a device for scar-
ing birds, guarding a baby while a young couple bathe, recovering a
diamond ring from a caravan involved in a crash, or even shoeing a
horse so well that it went on to win a race. Patrols hence have even
more reason than holidaymakers to hope for a fine weekend. . . .

If any part of the A A year may seem to lack highlights it is the late
summer and early autumn. There are a thousand things to be done, of
course, but it is hard to discern milestones here other than that this is
the season when a late swarm of bees has been discovered inside a
road service outfit. Even the succession of exhibitions, and of such
sporting events as the 'Varsity Match, the Boat Race, the Cup Final,
the Derby and Wimbledon, which give the signs department (and
perhaps the patrols, too, with their 'walkie talkie' control of parking)
particular problems from December to June, tails off a little now. But
the A A is as busy as ever, of course, even when it seems that half the
world is on holiday.

The next real landmark is the return of the weather map as the
leaves fall, the patrolmen don their oilskins, the days decline and the
press relations officers sharpen their pencils in readiness for the coming spate of releases on road conditions and other wintry subjects.
Misty mid-autumn produces another focal point in the Motor Show,
at which the Association contrives to shine a fresh light upon its
yearly activities. Meanwhile the foreign touring department remains
cheerful as it meets a secondary peak of enquiries from those lucky
enough to be escaping to southern beaches or Alpine snows, and army
manoeuvres bring their own problems of signposting.

By November those indefatigable sun seekers, the swallows, have
deserted London to follow their own mysterious radio beam somewhere between Brighton and Maidstone offices, and the pigeons

strutting on Leicester Square window sills look in on men engaged on a programme of consolidation. This is a time for reviewing situations, for stocktaking, and for considered retrospect. Hence information which may have accumulated in the touring departments during the summer rush is now digested, reports on foreign hotels are checked, and routes and town plans are revised and reprinted. (For a popular stretch of road, for instance, 30,000 route sections must be held in readiness for the next summer.) It is a time too for looking ahead – for planning the inclusion of more information in the handbook, maybe, or an extension of ship to shore radio services, or a new leaflet to carry on the A A's continual and altruistic campaign for road safety.

And still the pressure of routine work continues. In a single minute of a typical day now, A A experts may be giving advice on the tuning of a sports car, consulting with a committee on the landscape treatment of roads, answering a query from a hospital on the treatment for a patient who has swallowed upper cylinder lubricant, discussing a new radio mast, advising an enquirer on where he can get a back number of a motor catalogue, regretting that they cannot overhaul an electrical generating set, and counselling a barrister on circuit on how he should set about passing his driving test for a power assisted bicycle. In one hour now at Head Office alone 960 phone calls will be dealt with, 200 route sheets despatched, £9 spent on postage, 20 disbursements made under the free breakdown service, 700 letters dictated, 120 new members enrolled, 9 press cuttings taken, 40 accident claims and 30 police prosecutions dealt with; whilst out on the roads 16,000 miles have been covered by the Association's vehicles, 2 articles of lost property recovered, 15 injuries tended, 4 garages inspected, and 500 radio messages passed.

And because the rhythm of the information departments is the rhythm of the year itself, the men who have regarded as routine such queries as 'Where can I buy a gun-trained spaniel?', 'What is the best source of information on the state of Europe's roads in the twelfth century?', 'Who is the best manufacturer of garden netting in Holland?', 'When does the ghost walk in Canterbury cathedral?' or 'Where can I buy ten tons of waterworn Westmorland limestone?' have now special information to hand concerning arrangements for bonfire celebrations, Remembrance Sunday, the Lord Mayor's Show and – of course – hotels which are accepting advance reservations for the Christmas holidays.

And then, suddenly, the visitors entering Fanum House, London, notice a Christmas tree in the reception hall. It is December; the year is near to its end: and perhaps it is more appropriate to take leave of the good-willing A A at this season of goodwill than to follow it systematically through to the last week of its annual cycle. For Christmas Day is one day of the year on which all the Association's staff (except those who live and work in Scotland and the full emergency staffs who will in a dozen offices be eating their plum pudding amongst lights and telephone bells) are at rest – one day out of 365 when the A A is not rendering services to the public as unexpected and diverse as sending an engineer to repair the model railway of a foreign king, arranging for a lorry to move the equipment of a troop of boy scouts, presenting a bouquet of flowers to a member's wife at an airport, surveying a shop for a member interested in buying it, or hunting for a lost car in a dark wood at one o'clock in the morning.

It is Christmas Eve then; and for once the lights are going out early in Fanum Houses all over Britain, save in those operations rooms where a night breakdown call will be expected every twenty seconds. A dark and perhaps snow-impending evening covers Leicester Square, the spired and steepled cities of Exeter and Norwich, the conurbations of Birmingham and Manchester, such outposts as Edinburgh, Cardiff and Paris, the little port offices following the British coast and, indeed, all of the forty-seven centres of the A A. And, from all of these, senior executives and junior typists are homeward bound now.

Some, perhaps, will call in at a holly bedecked tavern for a quick convivial drink with colleagues. Some will even now be talking shop, or at least lightheartedly recalling the odder moments of the year –

the enquirer who wanted to drive to France over the 'Channel Bridge', for instance, or the tourist who asked the charge on the Woolwich Free Ferry. Some may be reminiscing over one of the most extraordinary examples of A A service of all, when an explorer near the south pole cabled Fanum House: PLEASE SETTLE ARGUMENT STOP FROM WHERE TO WHERE DO ROADS A7 AND A30 GO STOP CAN WE HAVE HANDBOOK TO SETTLE ARGUMENTS MORE CHEAPLY AND BADGE OR PENNANT FOR NANSEN SLEDGE PLEASE, and received within hours the Secretary's reply: HOPE FOLLOWING WILL RESTORE TRANQUILLITY STOP A7 CARLISLE TO EDINBURGH A30 HOUNSLOW TO LANDS END STOP HANDBOOK BADGE AND PENNANT BEING AIRMAILED STOP INVESTIGATING POSSIBILITIES OF BREAKDOWN SERVICE FOR HUSKIES. And some few, some very few, may have memories of those first distant piratical days of the great organisation which they now serve.

For these last there will be an especial significance in the fact that just one such year as has here been described was the golden jubilee year of the Automobile Association.

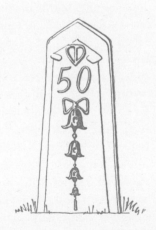

INDEX